Educational System
in a Globalized World

Educational System in a Globalized World

Best Practices In Teaching Online

Sofia Laurden Davis, PhD

To order additional copies of this book, contact:

Xlibris
844-714-8691
www.Xlibris.com
Orders@Xlibris.com
821919

This book can be ordered through author's website at
www.laurdendavis.com
Also send book inquiry to:
Sofia's Intellectual Property
P.O. Box 1211
Bonifay, Florida 32425

CONTENTS

ACKNOWLEDGEMENT

To everyone who is interested and chooses to take classes online and especially to those who are curious about educational system in a globalized world, faculty, students, colleges, and universities, and to all of my mentors at Northcentral University and my classmates online. Thank you.

INTRODUCTION

When we say 21st Century Students that means these individuals are apt and prepared to use the world's digital technology. These individuals are ready and have adapted the "Five Minds of the Future" by Gardner (2010). These 21st century students adapted: The disciplined mind, synthesizing mind, the creating mind, the respectful mind, and the ethical mind. We must call for a change to realign our educational system for 21st century students.

Educational system must adapt the technology changes to fit in with the need of 21st century students. Pearlman (2010) stated that we must design new learning environment to support 21st century skills emerging in technology. "If these changes are real, then schools are now enabled to move away from teacher-directed whole-group instruction to create learner centered workplaces for a collaborative culture of students at work. Many new schools designs in the United States and the United Kingdom have done this. A review of best practice illuminates these new 21st century learning environments and school facilities to help school designers and developers and education, civic, and business leaders launch the next generation of innovative schools" (p. 118). We must stress creativity, critical thinking, problem solving, communication, and so on that Brook (2012) stated we are to develop a constructive interactive classroom that would drawn students' interest in participating discussion (pp.1-2).

An online student's need is to be able to accomplish more responsibilities in a short period of time. Student's motivation in furthering education in an online environment can be the factors of for example, money savings for gas, car maintenance expense, spend more time with family, safety, and the availability of technology that allows student to multitask in a digital world. Being able to connect to the world through online learning environment is an experience that a learner would not have in a traditional learning environment. Advance technology enable online student to connect to the world learning environment with flexibility and less pressure. However, there are those individuals that are unable to catch up with the information surge and will be placed in the category of a traditional and hybrid learning.

Perhaps, complacency of adapting the 21st century skills due to unclear understanding what is 21st Century skills that 21st Century students must be armed with in this era of information surge in a digital world. For this idea, educational system may have to develop its own new policy to realign the needs for students of today.

CHAPTER 1

WHY ONLINE LEARNING AND ONLINE TEACHING?

The rise of virtual global classrooms will be very challenging to anyone. Whether we like it or not it is here and we must adapt and learn on how to communicate through digital technology, and globally. Richard (2010) stated that "We are now officially live in a world where even twelve-year olds can create their own global classrooms around the things about which they are most passionate (p.286). He continued, the world's digital technology possess complexity, pitfalls, and huge challenges to all educators. Therefore, in an online or distance learning, compilation of carefully crafted words is very important communication tool for the instructor and students to effectively relate the message. Instructor and student's knowledge in technology, self-discipline, and knowing how to communicate effectively is vital (Hege, 2011). Hege, (2011), in terms of issues of courses design, social presence, specially tailored assignments, learner's expectations, objectives, and a successful facilitation in an online learning environment, special attention to the relationship between technology and pedagogy is vital. Fisher and Frey (2010) stated through intentional instruction the focus is developing students' thinking skills which the significant part of their work providing students of support to be successful. Both continued, "The tools themselves evolve; our task as educators is to foreground communication while keeping abreast of the technologies that support it"(pp.223-230).

Every word counts in the absence of face-to-face interaction that communicating effectively in virtual world of technology is important. In writing a message, everyone of us goes through a process of realigning words in unity, coherence, errors that we can hear, and errors that we can see in order to relate and send an effective message to communicate well. In a virtual class, one of the formative assessments, "communication" is very much needed to understand what each has to say and to be heard. Berridge, G. G., Penney, S., & Wells, J. A. (2012) study of formative assessments of classroom teaching for online class are resource, communication, faculty-student interaction, assignments, grading and exams, instructional methods and materials, course outcomes, student effort and involvement, course difficulty, workload, and pace.

Although, students' technology difficulty resulted in mixed results of the study that in the future online class this could interfered learning. Berridge continued "As more and more classes and programs are offered online, quality of the delivery of those courses should be addressed. As more instructors accept responsibility for delivering online courses, new instruments and assessments needed to be developed to give instructors accurate feedback about their teaching methods" (p.127).

When a student unable to accept correction due to other responsibilities such as work and family, giving constructive criticism on his/her writing will help student rethink that crafting words through writing is an important communication in today's learning environment. In this era, a faculty must realize that student does multiple responsibilities called "multitask." It is not just the way how the words are processed and communicated but other responsibilities due to tasks at hand student takes on that realigning the writing is easy to leave unnoticed, and unimportant. Therefore, to gear student to think writing that an assignment and or a respond it is important to hear what has been delivered in the courseroom through crafted words. Faculty must keep in mind that student is there to learn and need guidance in a professional and a positive manner. In a way faculty's response must gear towards critical thinking to make the learner think that a piece of writing is a valuable method to convey a message. Therefore, reconstructing and revising a piece of writing is a way to convey a message effectively for the readers (Berridge, G. G., Penney, S., & Wells, J. A. 2012; and Kay, K., 2010).

Therefore, in an online learning e-reader, and e-library tools may be used by students to seek knowledge. Composition of words in instruction on how to use must be easy to understand and may have to be straight forward. In order to communicate effectively, the creator of these technologies must clearly convey the instruction. Similarly, students must learn to write a passage that is very easy to understand. For student to be interested in the subject, poor response will not be able to help student to think creatively. The Poor Response would create student's disinterest of the subject. Not only that Poor Response develops fear in writing, it also develops a communication boundary between student and faculty. The Poor Response creates hustle and hostile learning environment, and conveyed a negative message. The negative message creates the unprofessional stature for the instructor and the university.

The goal for 21st Century learning environment is to have students develop their skills in thinking, learning, working, communicating, collaborating, problem solving, and contributing effectively throughout their lives. These skills however are not unique to 21st Century but according to Kay, (2010) "these are rarely incorporated deliberately throughout the curriculum, nor are they routinely assessed. This status quo relegates these skills into the "nice to have" rather than the "must have" domain in education, which means they are taught unevenly (p.xx)." Therefore, the constructive response will help students develop their thinking skills, learning, working, communicate effectively, solve problem of their own in giving students a constructive criticism. The constructive response also creates a positive outlook, and professionalism is exercised for instructor and the university.

Dede (2010) mentioned in his page that "student acting autonomously is a major category for OECD that again, is contrary to the current culture of U.S. schooling. Similarly, the NCREL/Metiri framework stresses student "risk taking," but this is unlikely to be encouraged by many U.S. teachers unless special emphasis is put on this skill as crucial to 21st century work and citizenship" (p.67). In this way, perhaps this is the beginning of the implementation in development of the 21st century skills for the students. The constructive criticism that makes student think and develop the skills to solve problem to rethinking and communicating effectively is an important part of 21st century skills development.

To communicate effectively, facilitator must give a chance to have student develop their own self-discipline, skills in creative thinking, and problem solving. Giving a constructive criticism of their own writing gives them the power to reconstruct their thinking process in writing for a positive reason. As a teacher and a facilitator you have given the authority for the student to think positively, and develop a skill to resolve the situation which in this case is to communicate effectively through crafting a message through writing. Constructive response benefits the student tremendously and will enable the student to communicate effectively.

In the implementation process of the 21st Century skills curricula, there are those that we may encounter who may not be ready to wear many hats for the future. However, we as humans are capable of using our built-in skills to do multiple tasks. These built-in skills we have enable us to create ourselves in the future who we will become… which Gardner (2008) called it the creation of the "human enterprise." He continued, the usage of several multiple intelligence (MI) theory is a self policy rather than psychological policy cultivating the multiple intelligence of an individual. Therefore, the capability to function multiple responsibilities we now are wearing many hats for this generation that the continuing changes of technology allows us to become a student of "Five Minds of the Future" (Gardner, 2008).

The analysis of Gardner's textbook is that an individual has the capacity or must have the capacity to realign the thinking process and must wear many hats for this generation to be able to catch up with fast phase changes and surge of technology, the digital world. Because of the surge of information fast enough that an individual must learn to discipline the mind. He continued "Recognizing that nowadays one can no longer remain within one's shell or on one's home territory…" (p.3). In order to be successful in the 21st Century, we must possess skills needed to keep up with digital world by using the multiple intelligences (MI) theory mentioned in the book of Gardner, the five minds of the future: the disciplined, synthesizing, creating, ethical, and respectful minds.

The Table Below Highlighted the MI theory of Gardner:

The Five Minds of the Future by Gardner	Contents of Each Mind
The Disciplined Mind	Mastered one way of thinking, distinctive mode of cognition: scholarly discipline, craft, or profession (ten years to achieve and master this discipline)
The Synthesizing Mind	Understand and evaluates that information objectively and puts it together in ways that make sense to synthesizer and to the persons.

The Creating Mind	An individual would go "beyond existing knowledge and syntheses to pose new questions, offer new solutions, fashion work that stretch existing genres or configure new one" (p.156).
The Ethical Mind	Ponders the network of one's work and the needs and desires of the society in which one lives. Ethical mind is more abstract.
The Respectful Mind	Welcomes difference between human individuals and between human groups, tries to understand these "other" and seeks to work effectively with them.

Gardner, H.,(2008).

According to Bellanca and Brandt (2010) that in this millennium we are at the hand of 21st Century model for education that better prepare us for the demand of citizenship, college and careers (p. xiii). In today's technology it allows student to function and complete task faster than ever before. As we move along from distance learning through postal correspondence, television mass media, radio, and film to interactive technologies learners become mobile (Anderson, and Dron, 2011). Anderson, and Dron (2011) continued, "none of these generations has been eliminated over time: rather, the repertoire of options available to DE designer and learners has increased"(p.81). The question would be, what could be the next tools for distance learning student in the near future?

The article of Berridge (2012) stated that the effectiveness and advantage of online learning are those availability of course materials anytime, time spent with difficult areas of the course materials, bridging the virtual and real world, and more active in learning. Student of the 21st century tends to engage in higher learning skills such as problem solving (p. 120). The article of Casey and Evans (2011) stated the college student in the future will be those who grow up in digital world and participate in global economy (p.2). In contrast, Hege (2011) stated that in his class he recommended student to post self-reflection on reading to engage and connect with other students and the instructor. However, constant textbook reading and reflection posting about the weekly reading have created anxiety for students.

Dennen, & et.al., (2007), although communication differs in traditional and online classroom, communication policy is vital in both online and traditional learning environments. The difference is the use of communication tools by students and teachers. In an online learning environment student communicate differently in the course room than in a traditional learning environment. The communication practices in online learning environment uses tools such as telephones, email, and perhaps presentation and illustration. Unlike traditional learning environment uses face-to-face strategies with the benefit of teacher's presence. Therefore, effective communication polices has emerge for in an online learning environment.

Few examples, an online student is to evaluate teacher's effectiveness through survey, and email communication to be archived for quality-control measure in an online learning environment. Education must create a new model in the 21st century for students to catch up with the way we innovate, create, self-discipline, and decision making in a digital world (Dennen, et.al.,2007). The textbook of Bellanca and Brandt (2010) stated that the "world is changing and that we need a new model for education as well as new policies in the 21st century. We are now in the new phase of working and learning environment. Today's learner needs the 21st century skills, and so as the policies in education must keep up with these needs. The United States schools and students have not adopted the changing world as of yet that complacency can create barriers to students and business leaders. The framework of 21st century education is predicted to fit in with the need of learners. Through the development of 21st century skills to transform the changing landscape of educational systems and the way we are supposed to learn to fit in for tomorrow for some is still unclear. Therefore, complacency is still prominent.

Although all educational support system and professional learning support agreed that the change is vital for the economy, however we are still having difficulty transforming ourselves as one of those 21st century learners and educators. Complacency is still prominent in every educational systems, business and organizations. Why complacency? There could be many reasons why the educational system and other entities still in a complacent category. The hesitant to change, adopt and transform perhaps a very difficult one because it disturbs the 20th century box that most of us are very familiar with.

Therefore, transformation or change creates chaos in the lives of people and families who are affected by the change. Changes or transformation to some is challenging. The one who is able to adapt challenges and follow up with short and long term goals will succeed. There is no question that people and families will be affected by these changes. This is where the complacency comes in. For instance, fourteen states have adopted these changes and retooling their standard assessments to support 21st century skills outcomes. Bellanca and Brandt (2010) stated that "many of these states face daunting challenges" (p.xxv). We may say that change is good, and challenges are the massage of the mind. The challenges massage goes deeper and penetrate every corner of the brain such as we do need physical exercise so as our brain that the outcome is a good health.

The development of vision and partnership for 21st century skills offer holistic and systemic view. The question would be is of how can United States schools and students transform from 20th century workers and learners to be able and to acquire the 21st century skills that according to Bellanca and Brandt (2010) is on how to "reconceptualize and reinvigorate public education, bringing together all elements of 21st century student outcome and 21st century education support systems into a unified framework." However, it is premature for the U.S. to reshape infrastructure without clear and thorough articulation of the outcomes that students need (p.xiv). Below are the comparisons of themes, and education support systems by Bellanca and Brandt (2010).

21st Century Themes	21st Century Education Support Systems
o Global Awareness	o 21st Century Standards and Assessments
o Financial, Economic, Business, and Entrepreneurial Literacy	o 21st Century Curriculum and Instruction

o Civic Literacy	o 21st Century Professional Development
o Health Literacy	o 21st Century Learning Environments
o Environmental Literacy	

Bellanca, J., and Brandt, R., (2010)

The implementation of frameworks for 21st century skills, and its analysis on how diverse the 21st century skills and its lack of clarity can be problematic to each everyone involved. We must recognize that. Therefore, assessment in this category of problematic areas must be analyzed at first. That means, let us assess the consequences first on what could be the problem and who will be affected of the change. Gardner (2008) stated which she definitely agreed "Those who do not have a discipline, as well as sense of discipline, will either be without work or will work for someone who does" (p.28). By assessing the problematic areas and hesitancies of people involved perhaps, changes and transformation could create less stress in people's lives. Perhaps, individuals that are affected by the change are those individuals lacking human knowledge. Gardner truly sought how art, literature, and philosophy help people in understanding the needs of every human being, culture, business, global, and its economy. But these valuable curricula were taken out from our school system and therefore, human knowledge is off the table. We will not be surprise that today we are struggling to understand humanity and its needs, the need for 21st century skills for learners and workers.

Therefore, the question would be, how can we be able to solve and assist the formation of 21st century skills? Gardner (2008) continued, "In the absence of a strong demand for these topics on the part of consumers, it is incumbent on those with the responsibility of trustee to make sure that humanistically oriented fields are protected" (p. 29). Is neglecting human knowledge one of the major reasons we are having difficulty assessing 21st century skills for learners and workers in the future? However, we cannot go back in the past but to move on for the future. How can an individual be able to integrate the Five Minds of Gardner? Cultivating the Five Minds is an individual's choice and self-interest. Therefore, the question would be how these choices can be of interest of that individual? The Five Minds must be desired by individual with disciplines. So, do we need the stability of the mind before having the Five Minds to converge within that one individual? Therefore, we must have a healthy mind and beliefs in order to fulfill the transformation.

The author believes through adaptation of the "Five Minds for the Future" by Gardner, self transformation, experiences and education we will be able to transform 21st Century skills for workers and learners of today for the future of the economy in United States and the nations involved. However, the outcome may not be a 100% fulfilled because as she mentioned in the beginning, healthy minds and well self-disciplined individuals can be the only individuals who will prosper and succeed. Gardner added however, "too much discipline clashes with creativity; those who excel at syntheses are less likely to effect the most radical creative breakthroughs" (pp.29-30). Specification of the word "discipline" such as self-discipline and rules must be defined. Self creativity notates discipline, but rules and regulations can be the barrier of creativity.

By creating Human Enterprise we must be well self-discipline. Then, we may hope that these individuals who are well self-disciplined share their experiences to those who need it. It is then, that the educational systems and professionals must accept these new ways of learning. Therefore, those who are having difficulty to self-create, and to those unable to develop the human enterprise, we hope that professionals develop a specific program or curricula and must be ready to implement and train these types of individuals.

Online student become more mobile to perform multiple task due to technology. Technology allows online student to make it possible such as spending time with family, saves gas expense, and a feeling of being safe from what is going on in our school system today. However, to be able to adapt the Five Minds for the Future by Gardner, business leaders, workers and learners must transform themselves and set their minds to tackle challenges and implement 21st century skills in the forum and within ourselves to those who possess the well self-discipline attitude. Therefore, educational systems must reframe their organizations and realign 21st century policies that fit in for future students that these future students later on become the nation's best workers.

9

■ **_Definitions of Gardner's Five Minds of the Future:_**

○ **A Disciplined Mind** is able to master one way of thinking, destined to march to success, distinctive mode of cognition and specialization, knows how to work steadily over time to improve skills (Gardner 2008, p.11-12).

○ **A Synthesizing Mind** is able to survey a wide range of the sources. A Synthesizing Mind is able to decide what is important and worth paying attention. The Synthesizing Mind would gather information together in ways that make sense to oneself which ultimately make sense to other person as well. A Synthesizing Mind is a valued mind (Gardner, 2008, p. 13-14).

○ **The Creating Mind** thinks outside the box. The Creating Mind attempts new things and continually seeks for new ideas. A Creating Mind practices, pick themselves up after an apparent failure, and so on. Society gives specials honor to those rare individuals such as The Creating Mind whose innovations actually change the ideas and practices of the peers (Gardner 2008, p. 16).

○ **A Respectful Mind** welcomes the exposure of diverse persons and groups, wants to meet, get to know, and come to like individual. A Respectful Mind gives others the benefit of the doubt. The Respectful Mind displays initial trust, tries to form links, and avoids prejudicial judgment. "The respectful mind, however, starts with an assumptions that diversity is positive and that the world would be a better place if individuals sought to respect one another" (Gardner 2008, p.19-20).

○ **An Ethical Mind** is possessed of a mind that is ethical. An Ethical Mind abstractly is able to think of himself or herself. An Ethical Mind is able to ask, "What kind of a worker do I want to be? What kind of a citizen do I want to be?" An Ethical Mind is able to think about himself or herself in a universalistic manner (Gardner 2008, p. 22).

■ **_How Unique Aspects of the On-Line Learning Meet the Needs of 21st Century Students:_**

○ Implementation of Curricula Considerations
○ Defining instructional design

- o Awareness of medium of communication
- o Skills inherit in teach less, learn more
- o Teaching in ways that helps student learn without being taught.
- o Global skills of awareness and innovation: financial, economic, business, entrepreneurial,
- o civic, health, and wellness literacy.
- o Promote intrinsic interest in learning (Fogarty, and Pete, 2010, pp.98-99).

■ *Use of Professional Learning Communities Online:*

- o Partnership for 21st Century Skills
- o Support professional learning communities that enable educators to collaborate, share best practices, and integrate 21st century skills into classroom practice.
- o Develop professional learning communities for teachers.
- o Urge educators to encourage knowledge sharing among communities of practioners
  (DuFour & DuFour, 2010, pp.77-78).

■ *Using Online Webinars, Considering the Singapore Vision:*

- o 1)Vision for a Nation- Thinking school learning nation
- o 2) Vision for Education: Teach less, learn more
- o 3) Vision for Implementing: Tight, Loose, Tight
- o 4) Vision for Collaborative: Professional Learning Communities (Fogarty, and Pete, 2010, pp-97-108).

UNDERSTANDING TRADITIONAL AND ONLINE LEARNING AND TEACHING.

In the beginning traditional teaching was mainly the source of learning. Then online learning was created and "courses were mainly delivered via interactive TV before the program initiated its efforts to move course online at the turn of the century to meet the increasing demand"... (Zen, 2008, p. 3). Today, hybrid and pure online learning environment is created. Instructor implements and deliver courses through technology in an online setting. Instructor and students communicate through many types of technology in a distance learning, e-learning or online learning environment. The three generations of online environment captured the heart of professionals, instructors and students who are interested in flexibility, mobility, and accessibility of learning environment in a digital world of technology. In the fourth generation which many writers believe that the digital world will take over the way we learn these days that for student in the future of online learning environment the repertoire usage of learning in its flexibility will continue (Anderson, and Dron, 2011). Many were puzzled on how to use an online course and how it works whether online education can provide better quality education for learners (Zen, 2008). The table below is a comparison between online and face-to-face learning environment.

Delivery Component	Face-To-Face	On-Line	Impacts Teaching, Learning or Both
Location of Students	*Classroom or Field Site*	*Virtual/Infront of a computer*	*Both*
Online-Web, e-Learning Delivery	Classroom in the presence of an instructor	In front of laptop or computer, iPad, Smart phone, cell, Video, audio links	Flexibility, less pressure, fully access to digital world
Hybrid Delivery	Physical classroom, and virtual classroom, some face to face interaction with instructor.	Physical classroom and partly everywhere delivery	Partly access to digital world
Traditional Delivery	Building, classroom, face-to-face with instructor and classmates	Physical classroom	Some or no digital world access

(Zen, 2008)

THE SIMILARITIES BETWEEN ONLINE AND FACE-TO-FACE LEARNING ENVIRONMENT:

Thiede (2012) stated that teaching online technique is vital in online learning environment. Some of the tools to communicate use by online instructor in an online learning environment are the following: 1) discussion boards, 2)blogging, 3)simulation/case studies, 4)wiki, 5)video tapes, and 6) e-portfolio. The course room method delivery for distance learning environment deal with technologies we have available today. Distance learning environment consist of two types of learning delivery components, online and hybrid. The hybrid learning environment is a mixed delivery method of traditional and online activities, and hybrid student experience the combination of face-to-face and online lecture implementation. That means, there are times student must be in a physical classroom and sometimes the assignments and communication between student and instructor can be done in the computer using narrated words to communicate the message. According to Hollandsworth (2007), the two instructional strategies of hybrid combining to achieve the flexibility and consistency of online learning with concentrated learning...(p.39). Student enrolled in distance learning or online learning environment learn and do their assignments through the usage of technology in the digital world of today (Altalib, Dunfee, & et. al. (2002).

Brown, and Corkill (2004) stated that teaching courses without student and teacher face-to-face interaction the possible misunderstanding and misinterpretation of words delivery can be developed mistrust to both parties. The language delivery must be carefully developed in a manner that every word we use must be crafted with care not to be interpreted in the wrong direction that will be misunderstood. Online delivery of lecture and communication must be clear, and well organized. In an online classroom situation, instructor's expectation must be clearly written and well developed that each every student with diverse understanding, culture, and perceptions will be able to understand the written communication delivered.

THE DIFFERENCES BETWEEN ONLINE AND
FACE-TO-FACE LEARNING ENVIRONMENT:

In contrast, face-to-face classroom delivery has opportunity to interact with instructor face-to-face. Brown and Corkill (2004) stated, "Teaching a course where there is no face-to-face contact with the learner eliminates the unspoken language of non-verbal clues that teachers use to get a feel for their classroom" (p.1). In an online classroom, the course delivery will be through technology such as Blackboards. The communication in an online classroom will be communicated through discussion boards, blogging, wiki, video tapes and so on (Thiede (2012). Bawane and Spector (2009), "Online instructor need to take on multi-dimentional role and to be effective online educator they are required to possess a varied and wide range of competencies" (p. 383). However, roles and competencies in both face-to-face and online is not substantially different because listening skills are both important in face-to-face and online learning environment, but the demonstration of listening skills may vary base on the role as an online and/or face-to-face teaching (pp.383-384).

It is common that an online communication makes the distinction of emotions, and gesture in communicating with instructor or student through written words. The type of communication in an online learning environment may not connate the physical expression that our mind directly interprets and communicate through such body language. Therefore, in an online or distance learning, compilation of carefully crafted words is very important communication for both the teacher and student. In face-to-face learning environment however, student and teacher have the accessibility to communicate face-to-face with less words to say. Student and instructor in a face-to-face learning environment meet at the physical address to learn, accept, deliver, and implement lectures. The advantage of face-to-face is that some gestures can be the source to communicate the intention for the receiver that this gesture can be demonstrated and explained through body language. In an online learning however, that according to Brown and Corkill (2004) professional wants to teach online must be aware of the practice and apply curriculum concerns, the right classroom culture and instructional method.

Altalib, et. al. (2000) qualitative study for classroom room management in an online and traditional is given us the clarification of the difference between online and traditional classroom management. The result of their study was that instructor in an online classroom must:

- ○ Motivate and engage students in the learning experience
- ○ Monitor their progress
- ○ Administer assignments and exams
- ○ Encourage interaction and cooperative learning
- ○ Answer questions and ensure achievement
- ○ Maintain an orderly and stimulating learning environment for the student
- ○ Creating individualize learning as well as group learning
- ○ Fostering interaction among students and between the students and instructor
- ○ Giving and receiving assignment on-line, presenting engaging, interesting lessons,
- ○ Getting to know the students and their needs, reactions and abilities

The hypotheses of the study in teaching online will take more time and efforts for the instructor to prepare the online classroom in comparison to traditional teaching. Altalib, et. al, (2000) study however, shows a different result. The authors continued that study results was that the time spent for classroom preparation, and student and faculty interaction in an online and traditional are the same. In defining the hypotheses and the meaning of time spent was clarified. It was indicated that instructors tend to report spending more time online over traditional classes. Altalib, et.al., (2000) explains, "That means, however, indicate that instructors tend to report spending more time and effort in online classrooms. Zen (2008) stated "the effectiveness of online instruction is not determined by the technology we use but by the instructor's" ability to deliver the instruments for online setting (p.2).

Based on Altalib, et. al., (2000) study, there were some invalid reports due to the usage of surveys. McQuiggan (2012) and Thiede (2012) study stated that first time online instructors' initial teaching style would mostly use the traditional style. Therefore, professional development to prepare faculty to teach online is vital (McQuiggan, 2012, p.27-28). Governmental institutions such as national and state levels encourage, support, harness, and empower online learning environment (Thiede, 2012, p.136).

- ■ *Analyses and Thoughts About Online Learning:*

  - ○ What do you believe are the potential strengths and potential challenges of on-line learning as contrasted with face-to-face learning?

The potential challenges of on-line learning is the "know how" to perform the many types of digital delivery. The surge and constant changes of technology can be challenging to most of us. The difference between 20th century students and instructor versus 21st century student and instructors, the 21st century students and instructors have the capability and self-discipline to fit in the digital world of technology. Previous and 20th century students, workers, educational systems, and companies are still adjusting to fit in with 21st century skills that challenge us all. To that effect, challenges will not be limited to the 21st century students and workers as well. In contrast, face-to-face student has the benefit of teacher's presence, and traditional instructor spends less time to teach and preparation of instructional tools and delivery. The challenges of face-to-face instructional delivery will be that transformation phase and to keep up with the digital world of technology. For face-to-face students in the near future their skills will become obsolete.

There are differences between face-to-face and online learning environment in communication. It is common that an online communication makes the distinction of emotions, and gesture in communicating with instructor or student through written words. The types of communication in an online environment may not coincide with physical expression that our mind directly interprets and communicate traditionally through such body language. Therefore, in online or distance learning, compilation of carefully crafted words is very important communication tool for the instructor and students. Instructor and student's knowledge in technology and self-discipline is vital (Hege, 2011).

Hege, (2011), in terms of issues of course design, social presence, specially tailored assignments, learner's expectations, objectives, and a successful facilitation in an online learning environment, special attention to the relationship between technology and pedagogy is vital (p.13). Creative facilitator's strategies are needed to meet the needs of students in this generation and more generation to come. However, online instructors of today facing temptation of designing by replicating traditional classroom model that according to Hege (2011) as much as the contents, forms do indeed matter. He added, "writing the syllabus for an online course must include considerable reflection on the nature of online education and the most effective strategies for accomplishing the objectives of the course"… (p.14). Today, communication tools are provided by instructor or university to students who are registered in hybrid and online learning environment (Hollandsworth, 2007).

AN OVERVIEW OF COMMUNICATION IN A VIRTUAL PEDAGOGY:

The study of Jones (2011) stated that colleges' survey on courses online ranges from 100 percent students taking classes online. Therefore, the seat time in the classroom has been replaced with online coursework. Electronics and digital tools ranges from overhead projectors to virtual worlds are now used for instructors and students communication strategies. Student taking online courses will use Internet-based course management systems such as Blackboard and WebCT. Blackboard and WebCT are used for implementation courses online. Jones (2011) continued, "Tools for online teaching can be categorized based on whether the tools are synchronous" and asynchronous"(p.70). Web-based conferencing systems and text-based communication systems are used in an online learning environment. Instructor would combine technologies into one online location through Learning Management Systems (LMS) or CMS. Learning Management Systems are software programs with different tools and package that allow instructors to combine all courses. In addition, these tools such as Blackboard are paid by instructors or the institutions of service providing access to the open source systems called Sakai or Moodle. Moodle or Sakai are systems that are freely available to any users. Moodle and Sakai can be modified.

The core of education in an online environment is the interaction between learners and contents. Communication between students and faculty in an online learning environment involved technology that through collaboration using technology mentioned by allowing faculty and students access materials, readings, verbal instruction, other sources, and more. This type of system Jones (2011) added that"...learners to develop and use higher-order thinking skills to understand information and assess new knowledge" (p.71). Kupcynsky (2012) stated cooperate learning is considered to be a form of active learning that student enable to "engage in deep learning reshaping concepts and discovering new connections through the use of critical thinking skills" (p.85). Learning Management Systems or CMS through Blackboard and WebCT communications enable students and instructors to connect, implement, discover, and engage in online learning environment such as live chat, wiki, discussion board, and video conferencing are essentials in online learning and hybrid communication. So therefore, here we are welcoming the digital world of technology that according to Yenika-Agbaw, (2010) "E-learning, as exotic as the concept may sound, and/or as scary as it may seem, can be invigorating" (p.116).

IDENTIFICATION OF AT LEAST FOUR COMMUNICATION METHODS:

- There are many communication methods in online learning environment. In this section identification of the four communication methods are explained in a manner that we understood as of today. The four communication methods in an online learning are live chat, discussion board, video conferencing and wiki. Identification of each chosen four communication methods are explained below:

  ○ **Live Chat**: Live chat is synchronous digital communication that allows student and faculty converse precisely the same time at the same location in the online course room. Live chat also called an instant messaging (Thiede, 2012).
  ○ **Discussion board**: Asychrounous communication such as discussion board is another communication tool for student and faculty to communicate and exchange ideas. In Discussion Board, students and faculty do not need to be online at the same time to

participate in Discussion Board. Thiede (2012) stated "Once a student has written their assignment, the student then post this assignment online" (p.137) and instructor is able to respond and post the question to student in Discussion Board. Discussion Board's capabilities are: post and read assignment, take notes, critique and analyze the content, summarize various papers, draw conclusions, compare and contrast. Instructor and student will be able to comments over a period of time and the comments will be directed to the posting.

o **Wiki**: In creating a Web page content, Wiki is a tool that will enable the entire class to participate and be involved in a creative process, and freely collaboration through Web browser. "Wiki Page" is a single page of wiki Website interconnected by hyperlinks that invites student or students to create, edit, and collaborates group assignments or an assignment. However, this type of tool according to Theide (2012) could create a poor morale among the instructors and students.

o **Video conferencing**: Skype is an online video conferencing program that students and instructor will be able to engage in the course in real time. Instructor's introduction to the class can benefit students with a face-to-face interaction knowing each other's personality and each likes and dislikes (Hege, 2011).

EACH COMMUNICATION METHOD IDENTIFIED:

Live chat is a synchronous communication tool called instant messaging. Instructors and students use the discussion board to post, read assignment, take notes, critique, analyze the content, summarize various papers, draw conclusions, compare and contrast ideas. Using Wiki tool will enable the entire class to participate in creative process, and collaboration freely through Web browser. Video conferencing through Skype program is another tool to communicate with students with face and personality meeting.

EXAMPLES OF FOUR KINDS OF COMMUNICATIONS:

Based on the author's experience to present her final defense presentation for my dissertation, meeting with my mentor and committee members, She had to used PGi.com. She only paid $2.00 for just that day for an hour usage to present my final defense presentation with GlobalMeet sponsored by PGi.com. GlobalMeet can also be a source for communication between students and faculty. In teaching online, instructor will have to register through PGi and the fee is $65 a month or $500.00 a year for membership. The advantage of GlobalMeet is that a student will be able to present his/her PowerPoint presentation globally, and GlobalMeet is also available for group meeting all over the world. Currently, GlobalMeet is serving businesses, institutions, and individuals with the need of communicating all around the world. Maybe in the future, GlobalMeet will be available to serve anyone able to afford with smaller fee similar to Skype.

Another familiar communication is Skype. Skype is available to anyone who has the ability to download and capable of operating Facebook in the world of digital technology. Again, in the future perhaps there will be more gadgets to function in an online learning and teaching. Communication face-to-face with Skype is unlimited as long as student and instructor has a good internet connection. Today, if we dig deeper into the communication sources of technology we have available and are out there for now is free such as Viber to connect is to have a phone number and you dial that number and it will be connected through your computer, a computer with a WebCam. FaceTime is another communication that is similar to Skype. FaceTime can be used for one-on-one communication also FaceTime is able to accommodate group conversation. The author used "Messenger through Facebook which she has always use to talk with her son in Tallahassee Florida. "Messenger" is a one-on-one conversation by typing the words you intended to reach to the other end of the conversation. In addition, "Message" is like a ChatRoom and it is exclusive to one-on-one conversation only. "Message" can be used to connect around world. When it comes to privacy she is not sure if these features mentioned are secured. There are so many communications out there that are available, and student and instructor do not need to pay for it.

The author used the asynchronous communication tool such as the discussion board. Discussion board is a communication tool available of both previous Universities she went for her graduate studies. She would post her assignments, concerns, and comments in the discussion board area. Instructor will be able to response student's post and student is able to answer and ask question through discussion board (Thiede, 2012). To continue, the rise of virtual global classrooms will be very challenging to anyone. Whether we like it or not it is here and we must adapt and learn on how to communicate through digital technology, and globally. Richard (2010) stated that "We are now officially live in a world where even twelve-year olds can create their own global classrooms around the things about which they are most passionate (p.286). He continued, the world's digital technology posses complexity, pitfalls, and huge challenges to all educators.

Therefore, in an online or distance learning, compilation of carefully crafted words is very important communication tool for the instructor and students to effectively relate the message. Instructor and student's knowledge in technology, self-discipline, and knowing how to communicate effectively is vital (Hege, 2011). Hege, (2011). In terms of issues of courses design, social presence, specially tailored assignments, learner's expectations, objectives, and a successful facilitation in an online learning environment, special attention to the relationship between technology and pedagogy is vital. Fisher and Frey (2010) stated through intentional instruction the focus is developing students' thinking skills is the significant part of their works providing students of support to be successful. Both continued, "The tools themselves evolve; our task as educators is to foreground communication while keeping abreast of the technologies that support it" (pp.223-230).

Every word counts in the absence of face-to-face interaction that communicating effectively in virtual world of technology is important. In writing a message, everyone of us goes through a process of realigning words in unity, coherence, errors that we can hear, and errors that we can see in order to relate and send an effective message to communicate well. In a virtual class, one of the formative assessments, "communication" is very much needed to understand what each has to say and to be heard. Berridge, G. G., Penney, S., & Wells, J. A. (2012) study of formative assessments of classroom teaching for online class consist of the following: a) Resources, b) Communication, c) Faculty-student interaction, d) Assignments, grading and exams, e) Instructional methods and materials, f) Course outcomes, g) Student effort & involvement, h) Course difficulty, workload and pace.

The study results were mixed however, due to technology difficulty the technicality of the process interfered with learning. Berridge continued "As more and more classes and programs are offered online, quality of the delivery of those courses should be addressed. As more instructors accept responsibility for delivering online courses, new instruments and assessments needed to be developed to give instructors accurate feedback about their teaching methods" (p.127). When a student unable to accept correction due to other responsibilities such as work and family, giving constructive criticism on his/her writing will help student rethink that crafting words through writing is an important communication in today's learning environment.

In this era, a faculty must realize that student does multiple responsibilities called "multitask." It is not just the way how the words are processed and communicated but other responsibilities due to tasks at hand student takes on that realigning the writing is easy to leave unnoticed, and unimportant. Therefore, to gear student to think writing that an assignment and or a respond it is important to hear what has been delivered in the course-room through crafted words. Student is there to learn and need guidance. Instructor is there to guide student in a positive and professional manner. Keep in mind that instructor's response affects student's critical thinking. A piece of writing is a valuable method to convey a message. Effectively, for reader reconstructing and revising a piece of writing is a way to convey a message (Berridge, G. G., Penney, S., & Wells, J. A. 2012; and Kay, K., 2010).

EXAMPLE OF AN EMAIL LETTER FROM A STUDENT:

Dear Poor Response Faculty,

I was surprised by receiving so many comments. I have never had a problem with writing before, in fact have been told by past teachers that I am a very good writer. I don't see any mechanical errors in this paper and really don't have time to rewrite it before the final submission. I'm sure you understand that I have other classes and don't have time to devote time to revising a paper when there is nothing wrong with it." (NCU discussion example).

AN EXAMPLE OF A POOR RESPONSE TO THE STUDENT'S EMAIL:

Dear Student:

Your writing has to be revised and it is your responsibility or you will not pass this class. It is your choice whether to revise it or not, but I have to make a decision to give you a lower grade for this class. It is not my responsibility whether you have other classes to handle, but my responsibility is to guide and give you a chance to revise your work. You have few days left to revise your writing. If this writing of yours will not be revised your grade for this semester will plummet.

Sincerely,
Poor Response Faculty
A Poor Response Faculty

AN EXAMPLE OF A CONSTRUCTIVE RESPONSE TO THE STUDENT'S EMAIL:

Dear Student:

I do understand your concerns and your responsibilities for other classes you have that need your time and effort. You have great ideas in your writing and I am very interested to read your writing. However, I am having difficulty understanding and so as the future readers of your writing. The goal for clear writing is to convey your knowledge and creative work through words. I am very proud of you and I am very interested to comprehend your ideas through your writings. I am thankful for bringing your concerns to me. Let me know if there's any way I can help. I am here anytime you need me. I am thankful for sharing your wonderful ideas through writings.

Sincerely,
Constructive Response Faculty
A Constructive Response Faculty

UNDERSTANDING VIRTUAL, BRICK AND MORTAR CLASSROOMS:

Virtual Classroom:

The advantage of encountering conflicts in virtual classroom according to Walker (2004), students and instructor will be able to use their abilities to hear the voices of their colleagues through tone of voice in written words communicated within the virtual classroom or discussion room. Instructor is to participate in conflict resolution through normalizing strategy in the activity system program to resolve conflict and balance the discussion when conflict arises. The ***Activity System*** may need reshaping, balancing, correcting, focusing, analyzing, stabilizing, and it may need recommending strategies.

Brick and Mortar Classroom:

Students and teacher interaction in the classroom is motivated by active, and cooperative interaction that creates positive classroom climate. Heydenberk & et.al., (2007) stated, "Otherwise, the learning experience may be jeopardized by the presence of students who are not engaged in the learning process" (p.17). Therefore, incorporating social emotional learning strategies in cooperative learning and conflict resolution strategy in face-to-face classroom setting such as the I-statements, emotional awareness, and active listening must be implemented. Students are able to successfully resist prejudice and peer pressures as long as they are empowered with new social and cognitive skills, and students to avoiding destructive and deadly choices (Heydenberk, & et.al., 2007)

Interaction between students and teacher characterized as a positive classroom climate in discussion board. Motivated participants that interact actively and cooperatively may create positive classroom climate. However, in every classroom there will always be conflict between ideas of each participants or students. Therefore, cooperative learning and conflict resolution strategy in face-to-face classroom setting must "incorporate social-emotional learning strategies such as development of affective vocabulary, the I-statements, emotional awareness, and active listening. It must include with empowered new social and cognitive skills, student

24

are able to successfully resist prejudice and peer pressure when necessary, avoiding destructive, and sometimes deadly choices" (Heydenberk, & et.al., 2007, p. 18).

■ *Comprehensive conflict resolution programs incorporate social-emotional learning strategies such as development of affective vocabulary:*

- I-statement
- Emotional awareness
- Active learning

■ *Empowered* **with new social and cognitive skills, students are able to successfully**:

- Resist prejudice
- Be challenged through peer pressure,
- Acknowledge destructive behavior,
- Reject deadly choices and destructive decisions.

■ *Conflict resolution education:*

- Empowers students to resolve their own conflicts rather than relying on the external control from administrators of teachers.

■ *Students who are competent in conflict resolution skills are more:*

- Confident and feel a greater sense of psychological and physical safety in the school environments.

■ *Students in a comprehensive conflict resolution education feel more*:

- Confident
- Safer
- Have related increases in levels of school attachment.
- Provides the skills students need:

o   For increasing critical thinking, and comprehension.

■   *Positive classroom climate is characterized by* :

o   Active and cooperative interaction between a teacher and students who are motivated.

■   *Conflict resolution education provides the essential foundation for*:

o   Increasing school attachment
o   Cooperative interaction
o   Creating constructivist learning environments

In brick and mortar classroom, handling conflict differs than of virtual classroom. The advantage of encountering conflicts in virtual classroom according to Walker (2004), students and instructor will be able to use their abilities to hear the voices of their colleagues through tone of voice in written words communicated within the virtual classroom or discussion board.

In conflict resolution, this is the time students and instructor to participate in the conversation to resolve conflict. When conflict arise however, balance is the key. Thus, *Activity System* of the class has to be balanced. What is *Activity System*? Walker (2004) stated, activity system is based on what the study students are working on. It could be the entire course or a small group in the discussion board. The *Activity System* may need reshaping, balancing, correcting, focusing, analyzing, stabilizing, and it may need recommending strategies.

■   *Encountering Conflict & Nature of Conflict in Virtual Classroom:*

o   Sensory features are absent therefore it is difficult to manage
o   Through mediation, instructor may enter the conversation to resolve conflict
o   Discussion is off balance
o   Discussion of program study is disrupted

■ *<u>Understanding Activity System To Ensure Order:</u>*

o Expect positive and negative outcome due to
o Student's studying problem
o Negative outcome can be shifted if not corrected
o Other negative outcome may not be corrected but move to different type of activity or paradigm shift (Walker, 2004, p. 183.)
o Tool mediated system: Maybe use for conflict inquiry
o Instructor is to participate in creating a "cognitive map" for discussion within the course which is also called "culture practice"
o Concept of culture closely connect with culture that develop with them in Activity systems

■ *<u>Conflict Resolution/Normalizing Strategy Pattern:</u>*

o Complementing
o Generalizing
o Agreeing
o Dialogue to bring back discussion in line

■ *<u>Distributed Cognition Treats:</u>*

o Includes collaboration
o Encompasses both the individual and social
o Sees genres as just part of the real of study within distributed cognition and human activity.
o Encompassing activity theory and distributed cognition allow a broader look at learning environments and activities within them.

■ *<u>Distributed Cognitive Characteristics:</u>*

o Focus on physical environment
o Tools and individual as well as social environment
o Creates theory and distributed learning environment
o Analyzes and explains

■ *Understanding Normalizing Discourses:*

○ When tensions threaten the stability of an activity system distributed cognition analyzes it and normalizes discourses.
○ That means it repairs: linguistic or language repair
○ Tension is defined as overly harsh opinion expressed that hinders the free expression of ideas from other students.
○ Bringing the discussion in line

■ *Distributed Learning Environment:*

○ Student's location while participating in discussion board.
○ Computer or tools used in assignments, virtual libraries, etc.
○ Collaboration in other class
○ Esponses attempted

■ *Understanding Positive Dialogue in Discussion Room:*

○ Note: personal opinion does not invite or engage in a dialogue
○ Note: personal opinion does not invite the purpose of discussion
○ Create dialogue that bring back discussion in line
○ Dialogue must focus on the work

Cooperative learning benefits 21st century learners in developing critical thinking skills and problem solving, increase student motivation, cognitive development, increase knowledge creation and sharing academic success (Burdett, 2007, p. 56). In addition, 21st century learners will be able to develop skills to intervene positively, observe positively, and learn to handle controversial issues in discussion board. In managing conflict, 21st century learners would learn and benefit to minimize tension in the discussion board by agreeing, generalizing and complementing.

CHAPTER 2

ONLINE POLICIES AND OPTIONS: DEVELOP ONLINE

The communication practices in online learning environment uses tools to relate the message through telephones, blackboard, email, and perhaps illustration through presentation of the policies and instructions. Instructor and or student's evaluation report and its effectiveness through survey, and email communication are to be archived for quality-control measure in an online learning environment (Blair, 2012, p. 27). Therefore, effective communication polices emerged for an online learning environment. How do we develop policies for 21st century learning environment that affect students, faculty and the university it served? By understanding the needs of every student enrolled in the class to self-discipline and their capability to use technology in a positive and courteous manner.

Fisher and Frey (2010) findings include the National Council of Teachers of English (NCTE) with tools of technology they will be able to build relationships with others to solve problems and develop proficiency, collaboratively, and cross-culturally. However, educators facing challenges preparing students for economies and technologies that do not currently exist due to some negative beliefs of using technology. "As we consider the impact of our technology prohibition, we realized that we were doing a disservice to students" (p.227) American students will not develop a self-discipline or self-regulated skill as global citizens do who understood the power of responsibility that came with the technology. In addition "… it is likely that they will be required to participate on an increasingly diverse and global playing field made possible by communication tools that allow them to respond to social changes" (p.228). Thus, students must and will be able to:

> Design and share information for global communities to meet a variety of purposes;
> Manage, analyze, and synthesize multiple streams of simultaneous information;
> Create, critique, analyze, and evaluate multi-media texts; and attend to the ethical responsibilities required by these complex environments (p. 224).

Simpson's (2008) theory in self-determination maybe is the best requirement from individual taking distance learning. Student's study behavior to having freedom and flexibility Simpson called the role of "Autonomous Study Motivation Autonomy" which this freedom is promoted by choice. Therefore, participation in the process of learning and recognition of the leaner's feeling can be categorized as both negative and positive. Simpson (2008) added "Autonomous Study Motivation is contradicted by deadlines, surveillance, guild-invoking diktats and ignoring the learners' negative emotions" (p. 161). Educators must determine student's motivation goals on how effective it is to be an online student of 21st century learning environment.

Hu (2009) stated that participant or learner registered in Web-based distance learning has the opportunity to take classes with convenience and flexibility. While taking class online however, students enrolled in distance learning will have little or no supervision. Students that are interested to gear their continuing education through distance learning must have the skills to self-regulate. On pages 123-125, Hu (2009) outlined the skills of student to enroll in an online learning environment are the following:

- o   Due to high degree of student independence deriving from the instructor's physical absence, self-regulation is critical.
- o   Web-based curses and studies must address the use of self-regulated learning strategies
- o   Students are held more accountable for their own learning
- o   Student must cultivate the self-discipline to access the course communication tools on a regular basis to avoid falling behind with assignments.

Hu (2009) continued however, the attrition rate in an online learning environment is high in comparison to traditional learning environment. The predictor of achievement is self-regulatory behavior from student enrolled in an online learning environment. The reasons for being in high attrition rate in an online learning environment due to students lack of time and environment management skills, low self-motivation, lack of cognitive and individual learning strategies, low on self-efficacy on using technology, and discomfort of being an individual learner (p. 125).

Before enrollment process the University and Faculty in an online learning environment must be aware and knowledgeable the needs of pre-enrolled students of their knowledge on how to operate technology, and their usage of the digital world. An individual must answer questionnaires concerning self-discipline skills (Lemke, 2010). According to Lemke (2010) "The responsibility of educators is to ensure that today's students are ready to live, learn, work, and thrive in this high-tech, global, highly participatory world" (p.244).

In the article of Berridge, (2012) titled "eFact: Formative Assessment of Classroom Teaching for Online Classes" findings were very important for online learning environment rules and regulations. There are many variations of how students learn in online. Student's effective strategy taking online learning classes is base on student's ability to develop skills such as self-discipline. Berridge (2012) stated that the increase of students enrolled in an online is in fast pace due to flexibility and the opportunity of convenient learning opportunities. Berridge (2012) continued "Online courses are convenient and reach out to students who would not be able to come to a face-to-face class because of family, job obligations, proximity and other issues" (p.120). However, courtesy policy must apply to all technology users anywhere whether at home, in class traditional or online learning environment that interaction with one another must be in a positive and respectful ways (Fisher and Frey, 2010).

Berridge (2012) students' dissatisfaction in distance learning due to the following: technical problems, challenges of communicating effectively, and a need for more face-to-face interactions, lack of prompt feedback from instructors, ambiguous instructions for assignments, and technical problems. Berridge (2012) added that the comments from students about a new online degree program were categorized into five issues: program, course, communication, on-campus orientation, and technology.

NEW POLICIES FOR THE 21ST CENTURY:

Richard (2010) "Navigating Social Networks as Learning Tools on page 285 is an important message to all. "..learning—formal or informal—is no longer restricted to a particular place at a particular time. Individuals can learn anytime, anywhere, as long as they have access to the Web and, in turn, to other people with whom they can form groups" (p.289). Therefore, new policies in the 21st century should consist of rules and regulations focus on the need of students in the 21st century learning environment such as Hu and Simpson described in their study findings. Students are responsible of their studies such as the policy must consist of self-regulatory content. Because on Simpson's (2008) article stated that there are theories of learning motivation for students who are interested taking class online. Furthermore, Hu (2009) and Simpson (2008) research findings consisted of the 21st century policy gearing toward students and faculty to become independent and self-regulated individuals. Therefore, Fisher and Frey (2010) stated that

> Courtesy is a code that governs the expectations of social behavior. Each community or culture defines courtesy and the expectations for members of that community or culture. As a learning community, it is our responsibility to define courtesy and to live up to that definition. As a school community, we must hold one another and ourselves accountable for interactions that foster respect and trust (p.228).

To teach online effectively universities and faculty must acknowledge that some students entering distance learning maybe lack training and skills to be an effective online learner. Ineffective online learners may lack environment management skills, may have low self-motivation, lack of cognitive learning strategies, lack of individual learning strategies, discomfort with individual learning, and low of learner self-efficacy on using the technology for distance education program. Therefore, questionnaire must be administered to those who are interested to become an online learner and to be a faculty to facilitate in an online learning environment.

A SET OF INSTRUCTOR COURSE POLICIES:

■ *To Teach Effectively Policies:*

The "effectiveness of online instruction is not determined by the technology but by the instructor. An effective online instructor is one who is truly devoted to the success of the learner and who understands the dynamics of virtual learning" (Zen, 2008, p.2). Faculty must be knowledgeable of students' abilities, and capabilities on how to operate classroom technology. In gaining the knowledge on students' usage of digital global technology in a positive and courteous manner will help faculty determine how to help student realign in the course-room. An individual must answer questionnaires concerning self-discipline skills (Lemke (2010). Educators must determine student's motivation and goals on how effectively a student to be able to function in the 21st century distance learning environment. The responsibility of educators is to ensure that today's students are ready to live, learn, work, and thrive in this high-tech, global, highly participatory world. University and Faculty must develop and implement the Five Minds for the Future by "Gardner, 2008).

In order to hire an effective faculty member to facilitate curricula in an online class, the hiring responsible personnel in the University must ask question through questionnaires for faculty to be illegible as an online facilitator. Although student is an individual who is responsible of their learning and studies, but faculty must be able to assist students of their needs. Identifying faculty's ability and capability to facilitate online must be clearly stated. Effective and ineffective performance from faculty to facilitate online and accommodate student's need in a positive or negative manner affect University's reputation in an online learning environment. Therefore, questionnaires for faculty are highlighted below:

■ *Partnership for 21st Century Skills Questionnaire for Faculty in Online Learning Environment:*

○ How critical are you in grading student's assignment?
○ What bases of grading system you use to make decision in grading your student's assignment? Do you base your grading by having the student to develop problem solving strategy, thinking

skills, self-regulatory skills, and become curious to the subject assignment? Please write your response here:

○ Do you agree that essential skills should be infused throughout the 21st curriculum? Example: creativity and innovation; critical thinking and problem solving; communication and collaboration; information, media, and technology literacy; flexibility and adaptability; initiative and self-direction; social and cross-cultural skills; productivity and accountability; and leadership and responsibility (Hargreaves, (2010). Yes___No___Maybe___ You have a choice to write your response here:

○ How cognizant are you in a virtual class interaction with each learner and the wording of each message sent to those learners? Write your response here:

○ How knowledgeable are you to identify a variety of best-practice teaching techniques that are unique to the online classroom? Please write your response here:

○ How comfortable are you to include the use of emotion in virtual classroom, clarity of instruction, whole-class instructions, video and audio links, chat rooms, hands-on projects, assessing competencies and in-depth learning in online learning environment? Write your response here:

○ "Culture is just as important in an online environment as in a regular classroom. The classroom must have a welcoming feel to it. Learners should be challenged but not overwhelmed"(Brown, & et. al., 2004). How do you accommodate this type of learning environment for students? Please write your response here:

A SET OF STUDENT COURSE POLICIES:

The policy, rules and regulations for students taking online class must gear towards their needs and their capability to use technology. However, if student does not have the ability and capability to self-regulate, future students must be given the opportunity to attend training to be an online learner. Therefore, below are the questionnaires for student to measure their ability to be an online learner.

- ### ***Pre-Enrollment Questionnaire for Online Learner:***

- ○ Due to high degree of student independence deriving from the instructor's physical absence, self-regulation is critical. As a future online learner, how independent are you as an online student? Select 1 to 10 for your answer.
  1-3-No skill as independent learner
  4-6-Sort of but very low skills as independent learner
  7-10- Medium to high skills as independent learner

- ○ Our Web-based course studies address the use of self-regulated learning strategies. How is your skill as a self-regulatory online learner?
  1-3- Not self-regulated at all
  4-6- Sort of self-regulated individual
  7-10-Medium to high self-regulated individual

- ○ What are your strategies to be a self-regulatory student in an online learning environment? Please write your answer here:
- ○ Do you agree that as a student of an online learning environment you are held accountable for your own learning? Please write your reason if you do not agree.
- ○ How do you cultivate your self-discipline to access the course communication tools on a regular basis to avoid falling behind with assignments? Please write your response here:
- ○ How is your time
- ○ in taking classes online?
- ○ How is your time and environment management skills balancing job, home, family and learning online? Write your response here:
- ○ How is your motivation in taking online class? High__Low___ Medium____
- ○ How do you rate your cognitive learning strategies? High__Low__ Medium__
- ○ How confident are you to be an individual learner and what are your strategies to be an online learning individual? Write your reasoning here:
- ○ Are you uncomfortable to study individually? Write your reason here:

o How is your skill in using the technology for distance education program? Write your answer here:

- ***Yes or No Questionnaire for Pre-enrolled Online Student:***

o Are you a self-determined individual? Yes____ No____
o Are you motivated to take classes online? Yes__No____ How motivated are you? Write your response here:
o How motivated are you? Please select: Externally____ Introjected____Identified___Intrinsic___
o Are you prepared to reach your learning goals in a distance learning environment? Yes__No____
o Are you competence enough to use digital technology of today? Yes__No____

- **•*Positive Psychology-the Strengths Approach Theories of Self Questionnaire:***

o Are you a successful individual? ___Yes ___No __Maybe
o Have you experience success in your lifetime? Please write your response here:

INSTRUCTOR'S ASSESSMENT POLICY:

The set of instructor's policy through questionnaires is to determine whether the instructor has the ability and capability to transform her/himself to facilitate in an online learning environment for 21st century students. Student evaluates faculty's teaching methods through survey. Instructor's evaluation report by the students and its effectiveness through survey, and email communication is to be archived for quality-control measure in an online learning environment (Belair, 2012. p. 27). The Partnership for 21st Century Skills questionnaires will help University administration department to understand teaching method delivery by the faculty. Therefore, faculty can be assisted through recommendation in attending a Web-base course enhancing skills to teach online in asynchronous or synchronous training for faculty (Rukobo and et.al.,2012). On the other hand, the set of student course policies consists of information whether a student needs help in online learning environment and or how much help the student is needed can be determined by analyzing student's questionnaire responses.

CHAPTER 3

EXPLORING THE NEEDS OF 21ST CENTURY STUDENT

When we say 21st Century Students that means these individuals are apt and prepared to use the world's digital technology. These individuals are ready and have adapted the "Five Minds of the Future" by Gardner (2010). These 21st century students adapted: The disciplined mind, synthesizing mind, the creating mind, the respectful mind, and the ethical mind. We must call for a change to realign our educational system for 21st century students.

Educational system must adapt the technology changes to fit in with the need of 21st century students. Pearlman (2010) stated that we must design new learning environment to support 21st century skills emerging in technology. "If these changes are real, then schools are now enabled to move away from teacher-directed whole-group instruction to create learner centered workplaces for a collaborative culture of students at work. Many new schools design in the United States and the United Kingdom have done this. A review of best practice illuminates these new 21st century learning environments and school facilities to help school designers and developers and education, civic, and business leaders launch the next generation of innovative schools" (p. 118). We must stress creativity, critical thinking, problem solving, communication, and so on that Brook (2012) stated we are to develop a constructive interactive classroom that would drawn students' interest in participating discussion (pp.1-2).

According to Quillerous (2011) for distance teaching and learning the surge of new communication technologies development created difficulty to fulfill online students' assignments due to other family commitment and responsibilities. Giving students too many functions in the course room can be a time constrained for online students and faculty. Instead, be specific on what type of technology to be used depending on what type of course or subject that is offered. Quillerous (2011) continued "technological tools as the basis for the type of educational content supply" (p.180). Highlighted below are suggestions on ways to establish supportive online student environment. Wickersham & McGee (2008) ways to establish supportive online student environment are the following:

- o Instructional design should reflect clearly articulated assignments and expectations
- o Provision of appropriate instructional materials; prompt distribution of materials; clear description of evaluation and assessment processes
- o Present examples of expected and unacceptable behavior; level of assignment difficulty is determined by learners' level of competency.
- o Course content has relevancy to the learner's world
- o Customization in response to localize the needs of interests.
- o Instructor behavior requires that the instructor is responsive to learner's needs instruction is of the highest possible
- o Quality feedback must be provided in a timely manner, and feedback provide assistance in correcting behaviors
- o There should be a private means of communicating with the course instructor,
- o The instructor should provide positive feedback
- o Through appropriate interaction, the pace and flow of discussion should be responsive to learners and should be a productive activity to their achievement of course objectives.
- o Distance learning rely heavily on technology availability, and therefore the use of technology should be specific to student's needs.

Faculty's cooperative learning and conflict resolution skills are tools to support online student environment (Johnson, & Johnson, 2010, p.201). A faculty must be willing to listen and accept ideas and suggestions in a multicultural environment online with different types of learning styles. For effective online students who are self-regulated and self-directed however, faculty and the course room must provide questionnaires to know your online students' knowledge in technology and the their learning styles (Quillerous, 2011, p.179). Instructor must apply Deeper Learning Principles (DLP). That means, each learner's characteristics who "actively explores, reflects, and produces knowledge" is using DLP (Wickersham, & McGee, 2008, p.74). To design program that requires convenience to learner's satisfaction, it must be that instructional design is clearly articulated that means an instructor is responsive to learner's needs in social conditions, the students & instructor bridge to appropriate interaction (p.75). Through the right kinds of curricular designs is crucial to quality internet-based distance education program. The necessary academic and social engagement aspect made possible through the learner's desire in taking online classes (Chavez, 2007, p.2).

Creating a receptive multicultural online environment is to establish a diverse supportive distance learning in developing multicultural courses. The needs of this online environment must be examined to see to it that the need of this environment is fulfilled. According to Rasmussen, et. al., (2006). "The concepts related to diversity and multiculturalism can be taught in a variety of settings including academe, corporations, and the military. From an academic perspective, multiculturalism has been integrated into university curricula as required in undergraduate and graduate programs to enhance interaction and understanding between diverse groups of people"(p. 266). Chavez, (2007) stated, being knowledgeable of adult learner needs in online environment is a tool to create and establish multicultural supportive online environment. Chavez, (2007) continued, the importance of students' learning within a community where a credible level of social and academic interaction could be achieved due to globalization. That the benefit of most distance education programs in a diverse synergized community of learners must be at the heart of e-learning curricula developed for diverse community such as corporations, military, and other agencies are now educating their workers through online programs.

Thus, instructors explore how they can influence learning designs and scaffolding strategies of these types of diverse adult community of learners taking class online (p.1). In order to create and establish that environment for these types of learners online, Chavez listed the five assumptions about adult e-learners.

1) Adults are internally, versus externally, motivated about learning new things.
2) Adult students must transition from dependent learning towards self-directed learning.
3) Adults' greater reservoir of experience can be used as a learning tool.
4) Adults' readiness to learn is based on actual social engagement.
5) Adults need to apply for new knowledge and skills almost immediately (p.2).

■ ***Transition: Developing From Positive Face-to-Face Classroom to Positive Online Classroom Cultures:***

○ There may be no difference between face-to-face and online learning environment in developing positive face-to-face and positive online course rooms.

○ The difference between the two types of learning environments according to Wickersham and McGee (2008) that it is that deep learning principles must be applied.

○ When an online student has successfully and positively accomplished it is then that achievements have been revealed in an online learning environment.

○ Learner is satisfied when he or she is responsive to instructional design and instructor/peer feedback and action (pp. 78-81).

○ However, interaction can be situated in the instructional design and in other members of the online learning experience.

○ Within an interactive activity, if one or more students do not participate, then the experience of others is jeopardized. And yet, the individual's preference, styles or circumstance may determine how interaction engages the learner (p.81).

○ Seems multiculturalism and diversity in distance learning environments are possible in comparison to traditional face-to-face due to surge of technologies, and the community of adult learners and diverse community needs the flexibility in continuing their education.

○ The surge of new communication technologies development created difficulty for online students to fulfill assignments due to other family commitment and responsibilities. To establish a supportive, positive online learning environment can be beneficial to all involved such as instructors to students, students to students' interaction in the course room.

○ Specific technologies are to be used depending on the need of courses or subject taken by online student. In a diverse online setting, technology and course content must have relevancy to the learner's world.

○ In order to support positive globalized online learning environment for adult learners the needs in a multicultural, diverse setting, positive establishments have to be acknowledged and provided.

In an online collaboration, reading is significantly and independently related to course performance and it is an important activity for online learner to learner and learner to instructor or instructor to learner. Lifelong learning and its assessment consist of three "Rs" that according to Phelan's (2012) study that the resilience, resourcefulness, and reflection should be the contents of every online student's course of the program study. To facilitate effective learning the three "Rs" mentioned above are the most important components in an online learning environment (p.2). The complexity of online interaction within the computer-mediated activities lead to psychological and communication gaps must be overcome by appropriate teaching procedures are to be acknowledged in the 21st century online learning environment. The small group, and large group interaction such Dennen et. al., (2007) stated in the study that reciprocal interactions between learners to learners, learners to faculty, and faculty to learners are the most important communication as perceive by learners in an online learning environment. Dennen et. al., (2007) continued, other types of reciprocal interaction in online learning environment such as academic, collaborative, and interpersonal in addition to interactions in terms of function they serve are: direct instruction, social, and organizational.

Interaction by learner and instructor may lack elements of communication such as immediacy, tone of voice, and gesture. "Which teaching procedures are most appropriate to overcome the transactional distance vary according to the media used and learner's needs" (p. 66) depends on the medium use by learner and instructor whether in a small or large group in online learning environment. Therefore, curriculum and or course developer must acknowledge the type of program study, and the technology to use for a particular subject for online student's needs. In addition to conflicting study results of online discussion forum interaction and collaboration by student-to-student needs extended research.

Terms and Definitions by Dennen, et. al., (2007).

Lifelong assessment	important for developing students' judgments of their proficiency within the program of study as well as sustaining students' ability to assess for themselves beyond the program of study.

Sustainable Assessment	refer to lifelong assessment due to resonance with concept of sustainable development.
Beyond Summative	Certifying aims, the task supports the development of students' capacity for lifelong assessment.
Beyond Formative	Aiding learning aims, the task supports the development of students' capacity for lifelong assessment.
Assessment Task	is a supra disciplinary report, trialed in 2007 as part of a major review of two courses.

STUDENT-TO-STUDENT COLLABORATION:

Scholars turned their attention to the nature of interaction on instructional in an online learning environment. Online students' participation patterns across online and hybrid learning environment was the focus of Brook and Bippus' (2012) study. We may need to develop classroom format and or environmental design fit for every individual's needs in an online and blended learning environment. To differentiate collaboration between student-to-student in online, hybrid, and traditional learning- Brook and Bippus (2012) stated that these three types of learning environments varies depending on the student's preferences. For instance, adult learners mostly are enrolled in an online learning setting. Adult learners are constrained by work and family responsibilities. Particular student uniquely appeal and enroll in an online and blended called hybrid courses however, may elicit differential patterns of student's interaction which is the very factor that cause student to self-select specific course formats that affects course participation (p.2-3). Therefore, the difficulty of Brook and Bippu's (2012) study was that there was no perfect comparisons and comparisons were difficult to obtain "given the distinctness of each student group, physical atmosphere, teacher performance, and other factors... social dynamics of a classroom are difficult to "control" for the purposes of experimental study in natural settings" (p.6).

Fogarty and Pete (2010) study in Teach Less as a goal for the Singapore Vision, on curricula balloons with information therefore what should the student-to-student's collaboration be? Teach less by Fogarty and Pete (2010) stated that professional learning communities must address the Teach Less questions. Learning community must develop collaboration into a discussion that focus on the subject matter between students. Similarly, Hamann, et. al., (2009) study measured the value of online discussion participation. Weighing indicators of interaction between social behavior and cognitive gain or knowledge that social behavior in discussion posting may not be an interaction of subject knowledge. Asynchronous discussions analysis generally assumed that students' postings reflect and represent their cognitive processes and knowledge (p.9). Hamann et. al., (2009) findings stated that these assumptions may not be true for some students because there are many reasons why students unable or avoid discussion postings. This theory is no difference in face-to-face traditional classroom. Online learning discussion should reflect accurate reflection of students' cognitive processes. Course developer must differentiate social behavior and seeking cognitive gain and knowledge activities.

> It is not entirely clear at this point whether it is the fact that students read peer postings that links to better performance in the course, or whether the reading variable also measures other student attitudes and behaviors, such as a higher interest in the course, better study habits, or time-management skills. It is thus important to construct indicators and measurements of online learning that separate cognitive aspects from behavioral ones. Regardless of these unresolved issues, however our study has confirmed that student-to-student interaction in online courses benefits student learning and should thus be encouraged through course design (Hamann, et. al., 2009, pp.9-10).

SMALL GROUP COLLABORATION:

Small group collaboration help students enhance learning through communicating with other learners in the discussion room specific for greetings and course reflection conversation. Brook and Bippus (2012) study students were divided into three groups and invited to participate in the asynchronous discussion with assigned group members. For eleven online students enrolled in a specific class can be divided into 3-4 members. The group will introduce each other and discuss the subject assigned by their facilitator. The discussion goal will be towards the subject they are taking developed by the course instructor.

The discussion content must be an opening of an overall knowledge of the subject. If there is a need to have a conference with the group, the second discussion goal will be for conference participation. Conference participation will lead by the instructor. The discussion will focus on current technology usage, course room policies, and any concern about the program and subject. In the beginning of the class, if the group decided not to have a conference with the instructor, the instructor must send a questionnaire to each student. The questionnaire is a beginning assessment process for the instructor to assist student in the course room. However, the findings of Brook and Bippu (2012) study revealed no predictable pattern of group participation whether the class is in group size. It is that course formats are underpinned by social dynamic and relational performance (pp.4-5).

LARGE GROUP SHARING AND COLLABORATION:

It is that the significant innovations beginning to emerge in educational systems that we called online and hybrid or blended learning environment. Defining these two types of emerging educational systems such as pure online and traditional/online mixed is still in the process of realigning preferences and the research continues. Pearlman (2010) stated that what we see educational systems changes in the first wave of designing and developing programs in an online learning environment.

In addition to hybrid learning environment, hybrid or blended is slightly differ that full time online learning environment. Besides, building innovations of traditional classrooms appropriate for blended or hybrid course rooms, we are actively in the process of redesigning online course room and collaboration for small and large group of online and hybrid learners (p 118). As Fogarty and Pete (2010) stated the vision for education is to teach less, and learn more the integral to the first vision and speaks to the goal of teaching in ways that helps students learn without being taught (p.98). Collaboration between students can be one of learning without being taught. However, we are concern how important the type of collaboration between students in a small and large group. Does the group collaboration focus on the subject or program the group enrolled in?

> Fogarty and Pete (2010) continued, "Through the articulation process inherent in the PLCs, teachers in the TLLM Ignite Schools begin to look at the quantity/ quality issue through a different lens. While their system has traditionally compartmentalized the curriculum by disciplines that honor quantity of subject matter, they find that this structure can be deliberately shifted to focus on essential 21st century questions, conceptual themes, and life skills that honor the quality of student outcomes" (Fogarty and Pete, 2010, p.104).

In a class size of 100 students for instance, it is possible that only 50 students would participate in a conference or meeting of large group. Therefore, base on our example, fifty students can be divided into 5 groups for 10 students in each group. Blended class usually has a big enrollment of 100 or more students. In this scenario 5 conferences can be done for 50 students participating conference or meeting. Depending on the instructor's capability to handle number of students per conference also is an important decision to make by the instructor. In the case of all 100 students are interested to participate in a conference, instructor must develop 6 groups with 8-15 members in each group. Therefore, there will be 6 conferences to be offered within the class semester (Brooks, and Bippus 2012, p.4).

THE ROLES OF TEACHERS IN MONITORING AND ENCOURAGING ON-LINE COLLABORATION:

In the discussion board, learners are not concern about receiving a personal welcome or a response in the introduction of the program by instructor or the class (Dennen et. al., 2007, p.68). Dennen et. al., (2007) found that learner's expectation in the online learning are course expectations, assignments, objectives and in addition to upfront course information before the course starts. "Learners also want to develop a sense of the instructor's persona as it relates to the class…it has been found that, although instructor-learner interaction is important, not all students are looking for high levels of interaction, such as a response to every discussion board posting" (p. 68). The role of teacher in an online learning environment is to be a mentor, coach and a motivator. Online students are self-independent learners in online learning environment. Student selecting pure online learning environment has the skills of the Five Minds for the Future of Gardner: The disciplined mind, the synthesizing mind, the creating mind, the respectful mind, and the ethical mind (Gardner, 2010, pp.11-23). However, there are students who will choose to take online classes for experimental purposes such as if online learning environment is the right classroom for them. This type of student may will be become hybrid student or already a hybrid student. Therefore, we have two types of online students:

o The Gardner's ways
o Experimentational purposes only types of online students.

The role of teacher as a motivator that according to Simpson (2008) motivation is the central importance to online learners, and it is that motivation is not only a necessary condition for success but also must be a sufficient one. Online learners who are fully motivated "will overcome barriers of situation and time, and find ways of developing skills and be able to deal with the stress of study with very little extra external support-the independent learner's concept" (p.160). Simpson's (2008) four different types of self-concordance model of motivation that will help teacher to determine student's motivation level in an online learning environment:

o External-driven by outside forces.
o Introjected- acting in order to avoid guilt anxiety.
o Identified-based on subscription to the underlying values of the activity.
o Intrinsic-driven by curiosity and pleasure.

Another online teacher's approach to motivate online student is the use of "Positive Psychology and the Strength Approach" by Simpson (2008).

The Positive Psychology approach is a question of what makes online student happy, not what makes them miserable.

> Positive Psychology is the scientific study of optimal human functioning aims to discover and promote the factors that allow individuals to thrive. The Positive Psychology is the psychology of happiness, flow, and personal strengths. The Strengths' approach to learner support arises from findings from positive psychology… centres on enhancing learner motivation by emphasizing the importance of self-esteem as a vital factor in learning progress (Simpson, 2008, p.163).

Zen (2008) stated that to be an effective communicator is to reach out to learners early on. These types of communication strategies not only helps instructor's time as well as significantly help reduce students' anxiety. Communicating with students frequently and on a regular basis via email as well as through the website, and sending email for new announcement prefer learners for their next task in advance, and to keep students well informed. To be an effective online teacher and as a communicator is informational such as a teacher can be personal and emotional in order to help and establish a warm and supportive learning environment that is essential for student satisfaction and success in a class.

> An effective teacher send a "welcome letter, and a gentle private reminder, a note of encouragement, and a short thank you email to a making good progress helps raise the learner's confidence, and contribution to a discussion to inspire learner's desire to do an even better job. Positive relationship promotes learning and education would lose much of its value without such positive human interaction. Anyone who wants to be an effective online instructor should pay at least as much attention to these social and emotional aspects of communication as to other aspects (Zen, 2008, p.13).

The roles of teachers have shifted from classroom teaching to motivating, coaching, and mentoring called Facilitator in a diverse course room in an online learning environment. Technology and faculty with hand in hand approach and balance to have an effective teaching in online setting. Knowing students' capability in technology through survey will help instructor effectively assist student's needs in technology usage. Positive, constructive, and timely manner feedback for student's time and efforts accomplishing academic assignments and participating discussion is highly recommended for motivational purposes. As a facilitator, not a knowledge provider- effective feedback should aim at promoting interaction, facilitating, and collaboration (Zen, 2008, p. 15).

DESIGNING DISCUSSION BOARD:

The framework and purpose of discussion board has three components serving the communities of inquiry. The three components are: Social presence, cognitive presence, and teaching presence. These 3 extended components mentioned by Bliss and Lawrence (2009) found that overlaying interactions with peers, content, instructors, social, cognitive, and teaching presence are interactively proven and useable in the discussion board. Both continued that these activities are the important interaction and good practices for undergraduate education. Defining social presence in the discussion board may help understand how important social activities are to those students who may need social interaction from peers and instructor. Online students benefit from peer support networks for adult learners and distance learners that do not have traditional support networks than that of younger students' discussion board is important. "There are positive correlations between students' perceived learner-learner interactions and students' satisfaction with their online courses" (Bliss and Lawrence, 2009, p.1).

Small and large group development help educators to determine participants' behavior setting the course delivery participation. Asynchronous communication between students of online learners in a discussion board for small group design to develop practical strategies for designing and facilitating to increase value and provide learners place to interact (Jahng & Bullen, 2012, pp. 1-2). A positive collaboration relationship by students and instructor, and student-to-students the result is the quality of the learning experiences (Brindley, & et. al., 2009, p.2). Jahng and

Bullen (2012) examples such as whole class activity positive collaboration and participation scored higher. The collaboration and technology usage for a large group is divided into small groups. The example below illustrates the large group of 100 enrolled students divide it into 10 small groups. Jahng and Bullen (2012) added that the presence of the facilitator is very important, and both continued, "One of the difficulties in measuring discussion board activity revolves around multitude of factors which may affect discussion board activity" such as comparable results, course design, instructional approach, and learner specific characteristics (p. 18).

GENERAL COMPONENTS IN DESIGNING DISCUSSION BOARD:

The findings of course rationale and design considered highly important as the result of the study by O'Neill, & et.al, (2011). Practitioners and educators face challenges and difficulties to implement successful learning collaborative activities in an online learning environment due to emerging new technologies. Design and develop learning environments that appeal to multiple styles of distance learners in a variety of ways are the following:

- ■ *Technology Components in the Discussion Board: (O'Neill, & et.al.,2011).*

  - ○ Online forums and bulletin boards
  - ○ Asynchronous, synchronous discussion and chat functions
  - ○ VoIP such as skype, elluminate, and computer
  - ○ Collaborative document tools such as word document, and Google documents
  - ○ Email list server: email capability
  - ○ Social networking: facebook, wiki, Ning, facebook messenger, facetime, viber capabilities
  - ○ Podcasting
  - ○ Group conferencing: GotoMeeting.com with face to face capability, and synchronous audio/video/video conferencing capabilities.
  - ○ Blogs
  - ○ Calendar, agendas or schedules

- o Voting
- o Multi-user virtual environments (eg. Second life)

- ■ *Quality Collaboration Components in Discussion Board:(O'Neill, & et. al., 2011).*

- o Transform the inputs into outcomes
- o Produce genuine outcome of collaboration
- o Construct knowledge to generate through the collaboration process to complete a group task.
- o Sharing different levels of prior knowledge, experiences, personalities, and learning styles and attributes (age, gender, geographical location, etc.)
- o Transform the inputs into outcomes
- o Produce genuine outcome of collaboration
- o Sharing different levels of prior knowledge, experiences, personalities, and learning styles and attributes (age, gender, geographical location, etc.)
- o Participants should be able to expose written communication of individuals' participation in collaboration process.
- o Establish friendship, social relationships during the whole class discussions

STRUCTURE OF DISCUSSION BOARD FOR SPECIFIC GROUP:

Depending on how many students enrolled, large group will be divided into small groups, for instance: Enrolled students' counts of 100/10=10 students per group. The discussion board component of collaboration and technology for each small group of 10 students is explained below. As a reminder for course room developer that student would participate and communicate more in the discussion board when the student is merge with a group of active participants. Therefore, the importance of allocating student (s) is by mixing students with active participants (s). Through each student's participation behavior pattern, pairing student with active ones can be determined in the first whole class session (Jahng and Bullen, 2012, p.5). Whole class (large group) in the beginning determines active and inactive participants in the discussion room. By grouping inactive participants with active participants for collaboration will help students experience in a positive active interaction process.

The instructor's participation is when student active/inactive participations have been observed in whole class (large group) discussion board. This way, the instructor has the time to understand the participation behavior of every student. The instructor then is able to match inactive/ active participants in a small group (Jahng and Bullen, 2012). However, group size was not an important study of O'Neill, & et.al.,(2011) due to technology is now available for large group to work quietly well and allows students to collaborate in a large group. Similarly, the use of technology in a small and large group is the same.

> Developing a profile of the learner's knowledge, skills and experience, as well as their perceived needs will aid in the design and implementation of effective DE courses. Learner differences involve both the way that students will interact with the technology as well as affect the degree to which they will participate in online collaboration activities (O'Neill, & et. al., 2011, p.944.).

The role of technology of small group I chose will depend on the students' capability and availability by regions, belief, and geographical use of technology. O'Neill, & et al., (2011) agreed that "tools need to reflect the multiple styles for learning and not assume that students should adapt to purely linguistic ones. This doesn't mean we have to test and understand every student's primary learning style, only that we have to design environments that appeal to multiple styles in a variety of ways" (p.945).

SMALL GROUP DISCUSSION BOARD:

- **■** *Individuals' Participation*

  - ○ Whole Class Overall Activity
  - ○ Technology Usage explanation

- Announcement on quality collaboration participations outline
- Financial Aid/Finance
- Bio Forum
- Topic discussion forum
- Main forum (General Q & A)

■ ***Technology Components***

- VLE/Online forums and bulletin boards
- Asynchronous/synchronous discussion and chat functions
- Social networking software: facebook, wiki, viber, facetime
- VoIP such as skype, elluminate, and computer
- Group conferencing, GotoMeeting.com
- Collaborative document tools such as word document, and Google documents
- Email/list email server
- Podcasting

■ ***Collaboration Components***

- Construct knowledge to generate through the collaboration process to complete a group task.
- Sharing different levels of prior knowledge, experiences, personalities, and learning styles and attributes (age, gender, geographical location, etc.)
- Transform the inputs into outcomes
- Produce genuine outcome of collaboration
- Critical thinking skills development
- Co-creation of knowledge and meaning
- Reflection
- Transformative learning

■ ***Facilitator's Presence and Collaboration***

- Mentorship
- Coaching
- Facilitate
- Encourage students in involvement and participation
- Learner-centered courses: instructor to assume a facilitator role

■ <u>*Assessment of Discussion Board Activity by Bliss and Lawrence*</u>
   <u>*(2009)*</u>

- ○ Student participation
- ○ Quantity of student postings
- ○ Quality of student postings
- ○ Extend of threading
- ○ Instructor presence
- ○ Expectation and guidelines
- ○ Presence of feedback

The three components serving the communities of inquiry are explained in the introduction such as social presence, cognitive presence, and teaching presence. Discussion board is the place where students develop practical strategies throughout the interaction and collaboration of ideas. Quantitative/qualitative positive interaction and collaboration in the discussion board is productive and student-centered learning helps the group to learn through each other's input. Therefore, facilitator's presence in course room is an important one to make sure collaboration is geared towards productive interaction. A large group can be divided into small group to collaborate qualitatively and positively. Large group of discussion board activities in future research may resolve issues in assessing learner's characteristics, course design, and instructional approach. Designing effective distance education courses will depend on learner's knowledge, skills and experience and their needs. By being knowledgeable of student's needs and experiences will help course designer to develop and design an effective distance learning environment. In a variety of ways, we have to design learning environments that appeal to multiple styles.

<u>*DESIGNING MEANINGFUL DISCOURSE*</u>
<u>*FOR ONLINE STUDENTS:*</u>

First and foremost, perspective students plan to be an online learner must adapt the "Five Minds for the Future" by Gardner (2010). However, the skills for Five Minds for the Future by Gardner may take ten years or more to develop (p. 11). These five minds are: the disciplined mind, synthesizing mind, creating mind, respectful mind, and the ethical mind

(Gardner, 2008). Students would fall in between the Five Minds for the Future by Gardner (2008), therefore, meaningful discourse must be implemented to be successful in an online learning environment. Due to Distance Learning (DL) is convenient and self-regulated, many students globally are drawn to take online despite lack of technology skills and the Five Minds for the Future" by Gardner (2008). According to Zhang, & et. al., (2005) "Whichever the case may be, online learning requires careful structure, purpose, and understanding. Understanding student expectations is perhaps the first step to integrating online learning in distance education and establishing a model that will nurture a powerful learning environment for all" (p. 803).

On the other hand, Nair (2012) questioned on how we can help students that seem cannot make it or cannot pass the course due to inability to technology access, and unsuccessful to function in a distance learning. Nair (2012) study is given us an example of Open University in India. Success in distance learning cannot be achieved solely by any university that offers online course. Nair's (2012) study result of Open University stated that without the help of family, friends, and employer learner will be having difficulty to accomplish his/her education online because families, friends and employer are the people who constitutes the immediate environment for the learner. Nair (2012) continued, "The families, friends, and employer play a crucial role in either facilitating or de-facilitating the learner towards successfully completing the study" (p.324). Thus, understanding meaningful discourse for learner's success will be able to assist students who need help in distance learning environment. The question would be what constitutes meaningful discourse to help students need in distance education? Besides student's skills in technology, institution that offers course online may have to be knowledgeable of student's environment, stressors, workplace, and family unit situation.

WHAT CONSTITUTES MEANINGFUL DISCOURSE?:

As a University, a facilitator, and course room developer, how can we set up or establish meaningful discourse to distance learners? Nair (2012) suggested that these three schematic representations will help us to understand distance learners, needs. The three schematic representations of

Nair (2012) examined the following: 1) institution, 2) learner environment such as family, friends, work place, and society, and 3) learner's learning ability such as skills to function in a digital world. We may question, what can a university do for students to be successful in distance learning? A university must operate distant environment with a friendly approach through compilation of words and focus on enhancing learner satisfaction and minimizing student grievances.

How families, friends, workplace, and the society will be able to help the perspective student to be successful in distance learning? "High achievement needs can help in reducing the drop-out rate of distance learners" (Nair, 2012, p.324)? Nair (2012) have given us the examples of the second schematic approach:

- Provide required support such support as sharing responsibilities at home.
- Friends, workplace, and the society must motivate student in a positive way
- Learner's adequate skills must be needed such as high academic concept, self-concept, and achievement motivation

In similarity, Zhang, et.al.,(2005) study in regards to tutorial support in an open distance learning such as goals to meaningful discourse is to provide the students of the following:

- Provide tutorial support
- Flexible delivery
- Autonomous learning
- Ultimate goals for student's outcome and success

The questionnaires for enrolled students must contain questions that would help tutorial support, flexible delivery of online course, autonomous learning, and success for students taking online course. Therefore, educators' implementations on how to improve online tutorial support are those questions such as the following:

- What students' perceptions of using the internet for distance learning" geographically?

- How does this compare to students' perceptions of more conventional methods of students' support?
- How comfortable are students using technology for course purpose?
- What differences exist between students enrolled in English and or other language in an online course?

Tutorial Questionnaire to be Distributed by Nair, 2012.

Student's Perceptions of Using Computer and Internet	Students' Rationale for Using the Internet In Course Work	Students' Learning Strategies Used by the Tutor Online.
How comfortable are you using a computer?: 1-5	The internet makes it easy to find course-related information: 1-5	Is the tutorial given helps you in this course? Please explain:
How comfortable are you using email for communication?: 1-5	The internet makes it easy to communicate with the tutor:1-5	As an online student, what is your perception of the online tutorial support? Please explain:
How comfortable are you using the discussion board for communication?: 1-5	The internet makes it easy to communicate with other students:1-5	How do you access the internet? Please Check Choice (s):
How comfortable are you using chat room for communicating?:1-5	The internet is accessible and reflective:1-5	Home__Work__PC Lab at school__Public Library__Or You do not want to access internet at all_____
Are you having difficulty typing the language of instruction?: 1-5	I am efficient in using the internet:1-5	
	I enjoy working online:1-5	

IN WHAT WAYS CAN MEANINGFUL DISCOURSE BENEFIT A LEARNER?:

Understanding every learner's needs and life situation that Rhode (2009) suggested the three forms of interaction must be supported in a deep and meaningful formal learning is important. The three forms of interactions are: student-teacher; student-student; and student-content.

> No matter how one defines interaction, based on recent research it is clear that when the level of interaction is inadequate or nonexistent, learners often feel isolated and an overall degradation of the learning experience can take place. Conversely, the learning experience is enriched as learners engage in interactions within the learning environment that serve to scaffold the synthesis, evaluation, and application of knowledge. Interaction has been identified as a central component of such engaging learning environments and a catalyst for the development of thriving learning communities (Rhode 2009, p.2).

Questionnaire for tutorial should begin before the course starts. By being knowledgeable of student's needs before the beginning of the course in distance learning or online learning environment in addition to the walk through the course and internet usage are vital. Furthermore, study materials, counseling session, flexibility of delivery in an online distance learning system, and prompt schedule would benefit learners (Nair, 2012; Zhang, & et.al., 2005).We may question on how can instructors identify individual learner preferences in regard to discourse? We must analyze learner's life situation and each student's need such as the following:

Online Students De-Motivated Factors (Nair, 2012).

- o   Job pressure
- o   Family responsibilities
- o   Updating assignment grades
- o   Wrong entry of grades
- o   Result of examination delays

- o Delays of responses
- o Delays response from Universities queries and problems
- o Processing up to date information
- o Counselor not able to satisfactorily handle doubts

In the era of multitasking, students taking courses online preferred the convenient way of distance education. By taking courses online there is a flexibility of time especially to working adults continuing their education in an online environment. Students' preferences in taking online courses perhaps due to life situations, and the convenient as it may sounds. The institutions are to fulfill these needs by students in distance education setting. However, an institution will not be able to fulfill all students' needs because taking courses online a student must be a self-guided individual able to adapt the Five Minds of the Future by Gardner (2008). A student must be knowledgeable of the world digital technology. Without the capability and the ability to be a self-regulated, world digital technology savvy, disciplined mind, synthesizing mind, creating mind, respectful mind, and ethical mind, down the road there will be some trouble an online student will encounter. This is where the institution and the facilitator will come in and try to help online learner of their needs and understand his/her preferences. The instructor will identify these preferences. The instructor with have a role as a facilitator, motivator, and coach will then motivate and guide learner to move on and accomplish their task with the help of other students' collaboration in the discussion board. Therefore, how can online instructors increase the knowledge of meaningful discourse to accommodate online students?

Nair's (2012) Included the Advice for Learners to Successfully Complete their Study (p.332).

- o Prepare academic calendar and follow it systematically
- o Carefully read all communications from the OU and time-to-time seek out
- o information especially from the website
- o Make a sincere and concerted effort in preparing and writing your assignments which will to a great extent help in appearing for the examination.

○ Don't delay your studies, the more you delay-the lesser chance, you will go back and complete it.

Adapting the Five Minds for the Future by Gardner is a first and foremost skills and capability for student plan to take course online, but this type of skills will take ten years or more. However, we now face the surge of education that will be facilitated in a distance which what we called "distance or online learning environment." The very first choice among students is in online learning environment because it is convenient and self-regulated. To accommodate learners and understand their needs, Nair's (2012) schematic representations will be helpful for course developer, instructors, and the university providing the service in education. Institution that provides service and product to learner in distance learning environment must be knowledge of the important schematic presentation by Nair (2012) such as families, friends, work- place, society; and learner's learning ability and skills. Being knowledgeable of learners' needs will help course developer or instructor to develop a meaningful discourse.

To develop a strategy on how to help and accommodate student inability to function online is to be knowledgeable of student's life situation. To accommodate students, distance education may have to operate distant environment with a friendly approach through compilation of words and focus on enhancing learner satisfaction and minimizing student grievances. Enhance questionnaire for tutorial before course begins, knowledgeable of student's needs before the beginning of the course, a walk through the course and internet usage tailored study materials, counseling session, flexibility of delivery in an online distance learning system, and prompt schedule are vital. In addition, instructor must transform the role from instructor to a facilitator, motivator, and coach role enable students to learn a self-guided and independent knowledge seeking individuals through collaboration with other students and being able to use their thinking ability as a self-guided individual.

INITIATING MEANINGFUL DISCOURSE WITH GROUP:

- **■ *Advice Learners to Successfully Complete Their Studies (Nair, 2012).***

  - o Prepare academic calendar and follow it systematically.
  - o Careful read all communications from the university and time-to-time seek out information especially from the website.
  - o Make a sincere and concerted effort in preparing and writing your assignments which will to a great extent help in appearing for the examination.
  - o Don't delay your studies, the more you delay-the lesser chance, you will go back and complete it.

- **■ *Facilitator's Role:***

  - o Instructor should develop the course structure based on the course or program learning objectives.
  - o Designing the educational experience so that it is personally meaningful and educationally worthwhile.
  - o To determine whether learning has occurred and objectives have been accomplished, instructor must develop the tools.
  - o The goals must be clearly communicated to learners to help learners evaluate, monitor, and guide their own learning.
  - o For learners to become more self-reflective about what they have learned and what/why they have learned is relevant to the course, clear communication is important (Jones, 2011).

- **■ *Facilitator's Presence (Nair, 2012):***

  - o Being knowledgeable of student's de-motivated factors.
  - o Counselor's availability time and efforts to sort out de-motivated factors.
  - o Follow up on prompt responses from the University
  - o Prompt responses from facilitator
  - o Prompt responses in queries, and problems solving
  - o Provide tutorial support
  - o Flexible delivery

- o Autonomous learning
- o Ultimate goals for student's outcome and success
- o One-on-one qualitative, and positive phone call to assist student

■ *Group Dialog Facilitation Skills for Instructors:*

- o The core of education in an online environment is the interaction between learners and contents. However, communication between students and faculty in an online learning environment involved technology knowledge, qualitative, and positive interaction between students.
- o Through collaboration using technology faculty and students access materials, readings, and verbal instruction using positive and qualitative words in discussion board.
- o Educators provide both a basic foundation of knowledge and encourage learners to develop and use higher-order thinking skills to understand the information and assess new knowledge (Jones, 201, p.71).
- o In engaging small and large groups of students initiating meaningful online discourse instructors' capability to motivate, and coach students in a way for students to be successful in online learning environment.

■ *Group Dialog Facilitation Skills for Instructors:*

- o Communication is a vital component of teacher responsibilities and competent teachers must enter the virtual arena with tacit ability.
- o Facilitators must understand the limitations and appropriateness of various communication channels.
- o Effective communicators should recognize that phone calls can be used for a variety of communication practices.
- o Phone calls may be effective for reinforcing positive learning practices and updating families on general course information.
- o Telephone may be an effective pathway for decreasing the transactional distance in virtual school.

o Phone calls should be used in the beginning of a school term to help students recognize the teacher's voice and acclimate families to the school policies and procedures (Belair, 2012, p.26-27).

■ ***Group Dialog Facilitation Skills for Instructors****:*

o Apply within focus, and friendly approach to students in group dialog.
o A means for instructors to assess, reflect, and subsequently make changes to their own posting (Morgan, 2011).
o Identify three categories to describe instructor roles in online teaching—instructional design and organization, facilitation, and direct instruction—and their respective indicators.
o Assign inactive student with an active participant to learn from each other.
o Assessment of discussion board activity
o Facilitator to acknowledge that learners should not feel isolated in online learning environment (Rhode, 2009).

■ ***Ways to Establish an On-Line Presence Conducive to Group Discourse****:*

Facilitator's presence in online course and its interaction spaces through weekly readings, content, and weekly requirement to engage in asynchronous online discussions by being present, respond constructively, and draw students into discussion (Morgan, 2011).

o Mentorship, coaching, facilitate, encourage students in involvement and participation
o Develop task that includes group presentation, group paper, or other group activity (Jones, 2011).
o Defining the groups's composition to further manage the learning experience (Jones, 2011).
o Assessments: student participation, quantity, quality, extend of threading, expectation and guidelines.

- ***Processes to Create a Sense of Community in On-Line Settings:***

  - Instructors play a central role in creating the community of inquiry, and of which social presence, cognitive presence, and teaching presence are interdependent.
  - Understanding how culturally diverse online learning is and its lack of clarity can be problematic to each everyone involved (Bellanca, et.al., 2010).
  - 21st Century themes and education support systems
  - Global awareness
  - Online learning requires careful structure, purpose, and understanding (Zhang, & et.al., 2005).
  - Understanding high achievement needs can help in reducing the drop-out rate of distance learner.

- ***Processes to Create a Sense of Community in On-Line Settings:***

  - The three components of online presence: Social, cognitive and facilitating. Extensions of three components are: overlaying interactions with peers, and contents.
  - Asynchronous/asynchronous communication between students of online learners.
  - Develop positive collaboration and relationship to quality of learning experiences.
  - Posting reminder for students as "Online Community" (Morgan, 2011).
  - Keep in mind the difference between discussion forum as a place for developing community through interaction vs. a place for focused efforts towards completing activities (Morgan, 2011).
  - Sorting groups by major, student rank, or expertise in subject matter, and randomly assign student to groups for collaboration.
  - Examine how student interact with the media through which content is communicated
  - using two basic theories to identify and manage learners' interactions to maximize learning: *Objectivism* and *Constructivism* (Jones, 2011).
  - The investigation of virtual school communications such as *Techtrends* (Belair, M. 2012).

Preparedness in online teaching must be acknowledged and practiced by facilitator to meet special requirements due to certain challenges in facilitating course in online distance learning (ODL). Both students and facilitator or instructor will encounter changes of pedagogy, pattern in teaching, and course designing in online distance learning environment. Facilitator must also acknowledge that students enrolled in distance learning are older adults to young adults with diverse knowledge in technology (Baghdadi, 2011; Merrill, 2003).

DiPietro, Ferdig, and et. al., (2010) K-12 study findings for best practices based in Michigan K-12 schools explains the teacher's responsibilities and understanding between content and pedagogical knowledge from face-to-face to online learning environments which we called *"hybrid"* learning environment. The study results were twelve general characteristics, two classroom management strategies, and twenty-three pedagogical strategies. These findings were organized into five categories: community, technology, student engagement, meaningful content, and supporting & assessing students. Some of these findings can be applied to fully online learning environment.

Meanwhile, in the study of Ali, (2003) for online instruction and instructional design the concerns about quality learning can be replaced participants' attention center stage takes focus in the internet as an instructional medium. Online learning requires specific skills from students, and teacher. To achieve quality learning in online distance learning, being self-regulated individuals, skills on how to interact between teachers and learners, and skills in technology are the important factors in online learning environment. The driving factor for student-centered learning environment (ODL) is the changes in pedagogy. Ali (2003) explained, traditional is didactic differs than of a student-centered in online learning because the driving factor of e-learning is to change in pedagogy of teaching. Instructional delivery model in online distance learning environment promotes interaction learning, problem solving, and critical thinking. Therefore, the selected technology must be suitable for the learning objectives for learner, and the author stated, not every course is appropriate for online delivery, "Some courses require hands-on experience, making it difficult to provide such experience in a virtual environment because it will not have the desired effect" (p.43).

CHAPTER 4

ONLINE LEARNING SUCCESSFUL
INSTRUCTIONAL PRACTICES

■ ***Best Practices for Instructor or Facilitator's Roles and Interaction:***

One of facilitator's many rules is interaction. Due to ODL is lack of face-to-face interaction, delivery of scheduled time frame is important. Once class starts, facilitator has time to interact with students. Active participation serves as guidance, and manage student-teacher ratio and learner-centered in online course of establishing patterns of the activities can aid both students and instructor. Facilitators must be the content and resource expertise, online social process expertise, manager of the structure and process, and demonstrate technical competence with ICT.

■ ***Best Practices for Instructional Design, and Course Development:***

Facilitators are encouraged to develop their own curricula. However, collaboration with expertise, administrators, teachers, designers, and technical specialists are needed in designing and developing courses in online distance learning environment. A well-designed curriculum fit well in every discipline or courses. A well-designed course that will enable learners to develop appropriate proficiency and master within the specific discipline, therefore, curriculum should reflect the current state of the disciplines (Baghdadi, 2011).

- Types and level of courses
- Student interaction and course management
- Appropriateness of internet
- Course content
- Instructional styles
- Student skills and interest
- Access
- Quality control
- Time management
- Communication

■ *Best Practices for Administration: Integration of Curricula and Teachers*

Due to faculty's fear of perfecting high quality of online courses, programs and courses maybe created in many ways, but the resulting program created should be equally high in quality. For hybrid class, value on-site and online faculty equally and avoid playing off on-site classes against online classes. Create equally credible online and on-site courses and degree programs for hybrid. If faculty is in a different group such on-site and or online, set up a dialogue between on-site and online faculty. There are two keys factors integrated in these principles above: curricula and teacher. Therefore, highly qualified teachers, and sound curricula is ensuring best practice in online and hybrid (Baghdadi, 2011).

■ *Effective Facilitation Begins with Interactive Course Design (Merrill, 2003).*

Start with the process of designing a new course, or adapting an existing course, and develop rich, achievable, measurable learning objectives is important. Effective online course design and facilitation and develop a learner-centered model and for most adult educators, facilitator must be knowledgeable with the model for adult learners. Due to face-to-face absence in ODL, engaging voice and tone in facilitating a course create and effective visual presentation and effective online group (Merrill, 2003).

■ *Technology*

Facilitators or teacher must purposefully tie the use of tools built into the course environment to state benchmarks and standards to support student learning of content. When integrating web- based components into the course, teachers consider issues of student access to technology.

In addition, teachers must use the content knowledge and student's knowledge to drive the integration of technology in the discussion room. (Merrill, 2003) explains, the complexity of distance learning in technologies available of today's designer has more choices, and ways to deliver different types of methods in the course room. Technologies like Web 2.0 to use in facilitating a course can be in many forms such ICT, via computer, telephone, or radio, IM, text messages, online chat, listservs, online bulletin boards, blogs, and CMS or LMS.

■ *Learning Management Systems (LMS) or CMS*

Blackboard, WebCT, Angels and eCollege are some examples of LMS also called as CMS, course management systems. LMS or CMS consist of pages for announcement, syllabus, course documents, and calendar along with interactive features such as discussion forums, e-mail, chats, white boards, drop boxes and group workspaces. The system includes the instructional management featuring grade books, test construction and delivery. In addition, tools to connect digital library resources and other Web resources such as research databases, audio and video streams are part of the systems. Meanwhile, the Web conferencing systems are a more complex development that integrate synchronous video delivery, interactive white boards and chat interaction into online delivery. For example: Web conferencing systems include Macromedia's Breeze, Cisco's Meeting Place, and Live Meeting from Microsoft Office. However, Web conferencing is more often found in large-scale corporate training settings (Merrill, 2003).

■ *Pedagogical Strategies, Practices, and Assessments:*

Teachers use alternative and multiple strategies to assess students learning such as making course meaningful for students, providing support, assessments, engaging students with content, technology, community and communication, create student-centered learning environments for students that allow students the opportunity to represent their knowledge in ways that are personally meaningful, and teacher to accommodate the varying learning styles of their students.

■ *Engaging Student with Content:*

The teachers build in course components to reflect the interests of students enrolled in the course. Facilitators must be flexible in their use of pedagogical strategies to accommodate varying learning styles. Teachers establish strong relationships with mentors, and teachers use multiple strategies to form relationships that support rich interactions with students, motivate students by clearly organizing and structuring content, embed deadlines within the content structure to motivate students in self paced courses to complete course requirements, and provide students with multiple opportunities to engage content in ways that suit varying learning styles

■ ***Strategies in Making Course Meaningful for Students Practice****:*

Facilitators use strategies to connect and engage with students in conversations about the content and non-content related topics to form a relationship with each student. In addition, the facilitators are encourage to support communication between students and seek out and make available for variety of supplemental support tools to meet the diverse needs of students. In providing support, facilitators or teachers monitor student progress closely and interact with students to determine where gaps in knowledge may exist.

■ ***Communication & Community Strategy:***

Facilitator, or teachers facilitate the formation of community by encouraging content and non-content related conversations among students. Teachers interact with students using multiple channels of communication (telephone, IM, etc provide support. Teachers model what formal online communication looks like in discussion boards and emails. Teachers also must effectively monitor the tone and emotion of their communications with students.

DEVELOPING OUTSTANDING CULTURE AND INCORPORATING PRAISE IN ONLINE ENVIRONMENT:

Furthermore, developing outstanding culture in an online environment and incorporating praise to augment learner online engagement is the knowledge facilitator must possess in online teaching. The most important to being presence in distance learning is the participation in collaboration and interaction between student and instructor. An instructor to be able to transform into a facilitator of learning is a way to promote self-directed learning. Instructor or facilitator shows presence in distance learning is through discussion of course content, exercise teaching role, and fulfill student learning needs (Stone and Chapman 2006). These interactions mentioned are the significant contributors to student learning and satisfaction (Sher, 2009; Stone and Chapman, 2006).

Analyzing the article of Radovan (2011) however, shows us a different picture of a successful student taking online courses. In an online learning or distance learning environment, a student with self-discipline which Radovon (2011) called a "self-regulative learner" has characteristics of a well discipline individual when it comes to education and learning ability in an online learning environment. These types of individuals, the "self-regulative learners" set apart from the rest of online students. The non self-regulative learners may need constant attention and meaningful discourse implementation to be successful in an online learning environment (Nair, 2012). Since that issues in assisting students' needs may arise in online learning environment, the quality of discussion forum through analysis of discussion forum activities along with student focus group meetings studied by Nandi & et. al., (2012) clarifies the needs of all types of online students' needs, the self-regulative learners, and the non self-regulative learners. Nandi & et. al, (2012) stated "Our results show that students depend highly on the instructor's feedback and the participation of the students can only be evaluated with reference to be the moderation of the instructor" (p. 684). Instructor's presence in the discussion forum with student-to-student collaborations such students are the self-regulative learners and non self-regulative learners is important. Therefore, instructor presence through quality feedback is vital.

HOW CAN PRAISE BE USED TO IMPROVE THE QUALITY OF ON-LINE POSTINGS AND INTERACTIONS?:

First, let us analyze student-to-student collaboration and the invisibility of the right and wrong responses. This type of collaboration and interaction by students captured the deep learning of analyzing the subject they are studying. The collaboration about the subject enabled students to analyze their input by their own thoughts and the opinion of others. Meyer (2007) stated "This study provides some evidence that these graduate students could evaluate their own discussions without the instructor intruding or dictating an evaluation scheme, although this may not be true for other groups of online students" (p.1). Therefore, the role of feedback and students' judgments of co-students postings are important factors for students' motivation to post better postings and at the same time learning the subject they are studying. The role of online facilitator therefore is to motivate and coach students to participate discussion and collaboration by analyzing which posting is valuable, and poster holds valuable views, and which posters should be avoided (p.2). Qualitative posting can be enhanced and be elaborated within that collaboration to surface the main purpose of the subject matters which the subject of study through comments and praises.

Online teacher or moderator can also implement praise through the system recommended by Meyer (2007) such system as an online bulletin board to promote quality postings and discourage postings that are not valuable for the topic. The system called "Slashdot.org" is a bulletin board moderator used by teacher on face-to-face teaching. However, Meyer (2007) stated that "Therefore, it is not clear whether systems of evaluating postings, like the point system of Slashdot.org will work in online class discussion" due its directive manipulation of discouragement of those none valuable postings (Meyer, 2007; Wang, & et. al.,2010). Many studies results suggested that presence is an individual matter, linked to the teaching style, content delivery, and established patterns of instructor-student feedback. Stone and Chapman (2006) study of the eight ways of instructors' presence to be facilitated are explained below.

Stone and Chapman (2006) Structure of Eight Ways How to Give Feedback and Praises to Students in Online Learning Environment.

1) Via the instructor's role as provider of content and subject matter expert
2) By using materials that are unique to the instructor
3) Through the creation of one's own learning objects
4) By designing an effective student support structure
5) Through the instructor's role as facilitator of learning
6) By implementing high instructor immediacy behaviors in feedback (instructor to student interactions)

| 7) Through the use of a variety of media formats |
| 8) By organizing content and structuring the course for self-directed learning |

PERFORMANCE-FOCUSED PRAISE AND HOW TO USE OF SUCH PRAISE AND CAN BE IMPLEMENTED TO INCREASE STUDENT MOTIVATION?:

In the study of Radovan (2011) he pointed out the question of why student engage in learning and the use of learning strategies in addition to understanding and defining the concept of metacognition, defining executive control process such as planning, monitoring, control of cognitive strategies, and aspect of motivation. Radovan study result "theorists realized that reasons for academic failure, besides not using cognitive strategies, may stem from individuals' feelings about themselves as a student or feelings about a particular learning task" (p.216). Therefore, the finding for this study by Radovan (2011) was that for individual achievement the most important factor was motivation.

Dennen, 2005, and Meyer's 2007 articles concluded are given us the insight of how to analyze best and or valuable postings, and the not so valuable posting of students' in the discussion board such as "investigating the roles of some students in the collaborative learning process recognizes their importance in influencing the performance of other students. This does not negate the role of instructors, but it provides a necessary balance as both instructors and highly regarded students influence how the class proceeds" (Meyer, 2007, p.16). The following are the examples of specific performance to increase student motivation.

o In balancing between students' posting best and not so best, evaluation of postings and negating discussion towards the valuable ones.

o The role of investigation and influences of students and other students' performance and recognizes the value of postings through investigating the role of some students.

o Before final grade is calculated, finalizing the on-going evaluation process of best posts, and feedback with capability to bringing back the previous postings must be analyzed.

o Explore the use of other rules and praises to fruitful directions of collaboration such as allocating points of vote-getters, does points matter, and the use of Slashdot.org systems.

o Determining, and carefully exploring students' motivational needs, and or do students think that points matter?

o With younger students: Guide or direct students to instruction on what are best or valuable influences and to see what students would choose as best postings.

HOW DO ONLINE TEACHERS INCREASE STUDENT PARTICIPATION BY USING PRAISE?:

Dividing students into small groups for instance, 15 students to divide into 3 groups of fives would be able to helps facilitator to analyze the collaboration and interaction easily of each group. Therefore, the praise will be based by group effort (Brook & Bipuds,2012; Wise, & et. al., 2011). Partnering the inactive and active students and finding the way how each group accept praises whether points matter, points of vote-getters, and or whether to use Slashdot.org systems. Despite of student-to-student collaboration and the analysis for valuable postings, the meaningful discourse will be used to those students that are having difficulty through one-on-one attention with the facilitator (Nair, 2012). How to increase students' participation by using facilitator's praise?

Thus, the key to be successful is *"motivation."* Therefore, online teacher must transform himself or herself to be a facilitator that means is to become an individual to help bring about an outcome such as learning, productivity, and communication by providing an indirect and an unobtrusive assistance, guidance, and supervision to keep the discussion flowing smoothly to increase student participation through motivational positive praises (Brook & Bipods, 2012; Nair, 2012; Meyer 2007; Radovan 2012).

Most studies findings that motivation to learn is the most important for all online students to have. However, the importance of feedback and praises that represents instructor's presence in an online learning environment is important. Feedback influences the behavior of a system and its parts and that is governed by rules, such as questions as how online students felt about the postings that were the best or most valuable. Through these collaborations and postings analyses, the metacognition/cognitive control is exercised and implemented. The analysis of posters collaborations, feedback, and praises processes are exercised in an unobtrusive and an indirect supervision by the facilitator a thread of interactions towards metacognition and cognitive control. Thus, students'participations should have increased (Meyer, 2007; Radovan, 2011).

■ *In-Service Presentation: Creating Positive On-Line Environment and Rationale for Offering The In-Service:*

The overwhelming surge of digital world technology, and the needs for adults, working adults and younger students to transform their education setting from traditional to online learning environment.

- o The convenience of multitasking responsibilities and the growing needs of globalize learning environment.
- o Being knowledgeable of new transformation process from traditional to online environment called "hybrid" needs clarification for smooth transition to fully function in an online environment and hybrid.
- o Share the knowledge of positive online delivery, the implementation of meaningful discourses, and the deeper learning principles (DLP)
- o Exploring the online collaboration: Student-to-student collaboration, small and large group, teacher's roles in monitoring and encouraging online collaboration.
- o The surge and needs of new policies development and implementation processes in online learning environment.

■ *Exploring The Needs of 21ˢᵗ Century Students:*

- o Design new learning environment to support 21st century students' skills emerging in technology and support other students who need help in technology through meaningful discourse implementation.

o Schools to move away from teacher-directed whole-group instruction to create learner centered workplaces for a collaborative culture of students at work.

o Stress creativity, critical thinking, problem solving, communication, and develop a constructive interactive classroom that would drawn students' interest in participating discussion (Brook, & Bippus, 2012; Pearlman, 2010, pp.1-2).

o Exploring the role of instructor to transform into a facilitator.

■ *Establishing A Positive Online Culture:*

o Instructional design should reflect clearly articulated assignments and expectations.

o Provision of appropriate instructional materials; prompt distribution of materials; clear description of evaluation and assessment processes.

o Present examples of expected and unacceptable behavior; level of assignment difficulty is determine by learners' level of competency.

o Course content has relevancy to the learner's world.

o Distance learning rely heavily on technology availability, and therefore the use of technology should be specific to student's needs.

o Faculty's cooperative learning and conflict resolution skills are tools to support online student environment (Johnson, & Johnson, 2010, p.201).

o A faculty must be willing to listen and accept ideas and suggestions in a multicultural environment online with different types of learning styles.

o For effective online students who are self-regulated and self-directed, however, faculty and/or course room developer must provide questionnaires to know online students' knowledge in technology and their learning styles (Quillerous, 2011, p.179).

o Instructor must apply Deeper Learning Principles (DLP). That means, each learner's characteristics who "actively explores, reflects, and produces knowledge" is using DLP. (Wickersham, & McGee, 2008, p.74).

o To design program that requires convenience to learner's satisfaction, it must be that instructional design is clearly articulated that means an instructor is responsive to learner's needs, in social conditions, the students & instructor bridge to appropriate interaction (Wickersham, & McGee, 2008, p.74-75).

o   Through the right kinds of curricular designs is crucial to quality internet-based distance education program. The necessary academic and social engagement aspect made possible through the learner's desire in taking online classes (Chavez, 2007, p.2).

■ *Planning for Online Collaboration:*

o   The contents of program study in online learning and its assessments are: Resilience, Resourcefulness and Reflection.

o   The importance of reciprocal interactions between learners to learners, learners to faculty, and faculty to learners.

o   Other reciprocal interactions are academic, collaborative, interpersonal, and interaction in terms of function they serve such as direct instruction, social, and organizational (Dennen, et. al., 2007).

o   Division of large group into smaller ones. A collaboration with a teach less, learn more vision (Fogarty & Pete, 2010)

o   Focus on learners' expectations in collaboration: motivational approach. Teacher's roles as a mentor, coach, and motivator. Apply Positive Psychology and Strength Approach (Simpson, 2008).

o   An effective communication: Early communication with students. Positive and constructive and timely manner feedback to students' time and efforts. As a facilitator, not a knowledge provider-effective feedback should aim at promoting interaction, facilitating, and collaboration (Zen, 2008, p.15).

■ *Designing Discussion Board:*

o   Designing discussion board has three components: social presence, cognitive presence, and teaching presence (Bliss & Lawrence, 2009).

o   Development from large group to smaller groups would help educator determine participants' behavior in setting the course delivery participation.

- o Discussion board with asynchronous communication between students in a small group provides a place to interact and share ideas.
- o Positive collaboration by students-to-students and students-to-instructor result in a quality of learning experiences (Brindley, & et.al., 2009).
- o Keep in mind that the comparable results, course design, instructional approach, and learner specific characteristics revolves around multitude of factors may affect discussion board activity.
- o Design and develop online learning environments that appeal to multiple styles of distance learners in a variety of ways.

■ *General Components of Discussion Board (O'Neill, & et.al., 2011).*

- o Online forums and bulletin boards.
- o Asynchronous, synchronous discussion and chat functions VoIP such as skype, elluminate, and computer.
- o Collaborative document tools such as word document, and Google document.
- o Email list server: email capability.
- o Social networking: facebook, wiki, Ning, facebook messenger, facetime, viber capabilities.
- o Podcasting.
- o Group conferencing: GotoMeeting.com with face to face capability, and synchronous audio/video/video conferencing capabilities.
- o Blogs, calendar, agenda or schedule capabilities.
- o Voting, multi-user virtual environment

■ *Quality Components in Discussion Board Collaboration:*

- o Transform the inputs into outcomes
- o Produce genuine outcome of collaboration
- o Construct knowledge to generate through the collaboration process to complete a group task.
- o Sharing different levels of prior knowledge, experiences, personalities, and learning styles and attributes (age, gender, geographical location, etc.).

o   Participants should be able to expose written communication of individuals' participation in collaboration process.
o   Establish friendship, social relationships during the whole class discussions
o   Reflection, Co-creation of knowledge and meaning
o   Critical thinking skills development and Transformative learning
o   Assessment of Discussion Board Activity: Student participation and quantity of student postings, extending of threading, instructor presence, expectation and guidelines, presence of feedback (Bliss and Lawrence, 2009).

RECOMMENDING GUIDELINES FOR MEANINGFUL DISCOURSE:

■   ***The three meaningful discourses to understand learner's needs to be successful in distance learning are: Institution, learner's environment, and learner's learning ability and skills in digital world technology.***

o   Institution: university to operate distant learning with a friendly approach and focus on enhancing learner satisfaction and minimizing student grievances.
o   Learner's environment: family, friends, society, and workplace.
o   Learner's skills, and ability: digital technology, and Five Minds for Future by Gardner (2010).

■   ***Tutorial support, flexible delivery, autonomous learning, ultimate goals for student's outcome and success.***

o   Be knowledgeable of student's de-motivated factors: job pressure, family responsibilities, updating assignments grades, wrong entry of grades, result of examination delays, delays of responses such queries and problems from instructor and the university, delays of counseling, and information processing.

■ **_Incorporating Praise To Augment Learners Online Engagement Guilde:_**

o Partner active and inactive students to collaborate.
o Break large group into smaller ones.
o Use Slashdot.org system or other systems that you are comfortable to evaluate interaction between students.
o Facilitator to develop a "motivational" strategy that fit with students' needs.
o Balancing students' posting from best and not so best and negate discussion towards the valuable ones.
o Determine and carefully explore students' motivational needs and if points matter.
o Guide and direct younger students to instruction and postings on what are the best, and valuable.

■ **_Observable Analytic Rubric Criteria:_**

o Undergraduates:Through categorizing interaction, collaboration and valuable contribution in the discussion area in addition to individual's assignment criteria.
o *Undergranduates:* Student's ability in digital world of technology, and the ability to adapt the Five Minds for the Future by Gardener (2010).
o *Undergraduates/Graduates*: The student's skills of quality, positivity, creativity, cognitive, critical thinking, productivity, value of collaboration and interaction of postings and assignments.
o *Graduates:* Adapted the digital world of technology, self-regulated individuals, adapted the Five Minds for the Future by Gardner (2010).

■ **_Follow Up Meeting:De-briefing Questions:_**

o What did you learn about the In-Service Presentation?
o How do you transform your traditional current class to hybrid?
o How do you transform your hybrid class to facilitate fully online?
o What are the assessments for online students needing help to be successful in distance learning?

- What are the meaningful discourses to be implemented as a facilitator?
- What role do you play as a facilitator?
- What's the difference between instructor and facilitator? As a facilitator, how do you transform your students to use critical thinking skills the deeper learning principles?
- How do you base your judgments in regards to valuable and best collaboration and interaction in discussion room.
- To communicate effectively, facilitator must give a chance to have student develop their own self-discipline, skills in creative thinking, and problem solving.
- Giving a constructive criticism of their own writing gives them the power to reconstruct their thinking process in writing for a positive reason.
- As a teacher or facilitator you have given the authority for the student to think positively, and develop a skill to resolve the situation which in this case is to communicate effectively through crafting a message through writing.
- Constructive response benefits the student tremendously and will enable the student to communicate effectively.

IN CONCLUSION

First and foremost skills and capability for student taking classes online is to be adaptive of the five minds for the future by Gardner that will take at least ten or more years to develop. The surge of online distance learning is popular due to convenience and self-regulated. The knowledge of importance in schematic presentation is valuable for course developers, instructors, and the institution. In taking consideration of the importance of schematic presentation such as the learner's ability in learning and skills, families, friends, work- place, and the society in order to develop a meaningful discourse (Nair, 2012). Thus, policies and procedures must fit in the need for this generation; the adaptation of Gardner's Five Minds for the Future is a must skill for 21st Century society, students, corporations and institutions. To be successful in a globalized world educational system we must switch our thinking process to new practices for all.

SHORT FORM GUIDE FOR BEST PRACTICES TEACHING AND LEARNING ONLINE IN A GLOBALIZED WORLD

Best Practices for Instructor or Facilitator's Roles and Interaction

- Must have the ability to be a facilitator and ability to play its interaction roles
- Delivery ability of scheduled time frame
- Able and ability to participate actively
- Serves as guidance for students locally and globally
- Able to manage student-teacher ratio and learner-centered in online courses
- Ability to establish patterns of activities to aid both aid students and instructor.
- Ability of facilitators to be the *EXPERT* in content, resources, online social process, manager of structure process, and demonstrate technical competence with ICT.
- *Intellectual Role:* Encourages a high level of students' responses. To do so, key point is synthesized, and intellectual climate is nurtured.
- *Pedagogical Role:* Ability to transform from teacher to facilitator role.
- *Technical Role:* Ability to understand the basic knowledge of technology application such as Web 2.0 internet software, and specific technology need for each student (Ormiston, 2011).
- Ability to consider the importance of social and cognitive goals (Maurino, et. al. 2008).

Best Practices for Instructional Design, and Course Development

- Facilitators are encouraged to develop their own curricula.
- Facilitator must collaborate with expertise, administrators, teachers, designers and technical specialists are needed in designing and developing courses in online distance learning environment.
- A well designed curriculum fit well in every discipline or courses.
- A well designed course that will enable learners to develop appropriate proficiency and master within the specific discipline,

therefore, curriculum should reflect the current state of the disciplines (Baghdadi, 2011).

- Student interaction and course management
- Appropriateness of internet
- Course content, and instructional styles
- Student skills and interest
- Access, and Quality control
- Time management, Communication

Best Practices for Administration: Integration of Curricula and Teachers

- Perfecting facilitator's high quality of online courses, programs and courses maybe created in many ways, and it should be created in equally high in quality.
- For hybrid class, value on-site and online faculty equally and avoid playing off on-site classes against online classes.
- Create equally credible online and on-site courses and degree programs for hybrid. If faculty is in a different group such on-site and or online, set up a dialogue between on-site and online faculty.
- There are two keys factors integrated in these principles above: curricula and teacher. Therefore, highly qualified teachers, and sound curricula is ensuring best practice in online and hybrid (Baghdadi, 2011).

Effective Facilitation Begins with Interactive Course Design

- Start with the process of designing a new course, or adapting an existing course, and develop rich, achievable, measurable learning objectives is important.
- Effective online course design and facilitation and develop a learner-centered model and for most adult educators, facilitator must be knowledgeable with the model for adult learners.
- Due to face-to-face absence in ODL, engaging voice and tone in facilitating a course create and effective visual presentation and effective online group (Merrill, 2003).

Technology

- Facilitators or teacher must purposefully tie the use of tools built into the course environment to state benchmarks and standards to support student learning of content.
- When integrating web based components into the course, teachers consider issues of student access to technology.
- Facilitators must use the content knowledge and student's knowledge to drive the integration of technology in the discussion room.
- Facilitator/designer must be able to explains the complexity of distance learning in technologies available
- Facilitator/designer has more choices, and ways to deliver different types of methods in the course room (Merrill, 2003).
- Technologies like Web 2.0 to use in facilitating a course can be in many forms such ICT, via computer, telephone, or radio, IM, text messages, online chat, listservs, online bulletin boards, blogs, and CMS or LMS.

Knowledgeable of Learning Management Systems (LMS) or CMS

- Blackboard, WebCT, Angels and eCollege are some examples of LMS also called as CMS, Course Management Systems. LMS or CMS consist of pages for announcement, syllabus, course documents, and calendar along with interactive features such as discussion forums, e-mail, chats, white boards, drop boxes and group workspaces.
- The system includes the instructional management featuring grade books, test construction and delivery. In addition, tools to connect digital library resources and other Web resources such as research databases, audio and video streams are part of the systems.
- Web conferencing systems are a more complex development that integrate synchronous video delivery, interactive white boards and chat interaction into online delivery. For example: Web conferencing systems include Macromedia's Breeze, Cisco's Meeting Place, and Live Meeting from Microsoft Office.
- Web conferencing is more often found in large-scale corporate training settings (Merrill, 2003).

Pedagogical Strategies, Practices, and Assessments.

- Teachers use alternative and multiple strategies to assess students learning
- Making course meaningful for students
- Providing support, assessments, engaging students with content, technology, community and communication.
- Create student-centered learning environments for students that allow students the opportunity to represent their knowledge in ways that are personally meaningful.
- Teacher to accommodate the varying learning styles of their students.
- Teacher is to use assessment to focus on critical "thinking rather than on evaluating or measuring rote knowledge" and observation using tools of assessment such as checklist or portfolio (Pappas, 2007, p.22).
- Facilitator able to demonstrate formative assessment and summative assessment. a)*Formative Assessment*: Takes place throughout learning activity, b). *Summative Assessment*: Assess student at the end of learning activity. (Pappas, 2007).

Engaging Students with Contents

- Facilitator will build course components to reflect the interests of students enrolled in the course.
- Facilitators must be flexible in their use of pedagogical strategies to accommodate varying learning styles.
- Facilitator establish strong relationships with mentors, and teachers use multiple strategies to form relationships that support rich interactions with students,.
- Motivate students by clearly organizing and structuring content.
- Embed deadlines within the content structure to motivate students in self paced courses to complete course requirements.
- Provide students with multiple opportunities to engage content in ways that suit varying learning styles
- Facilitator's *ability to depersonalize message* using text medium that needs to be critically thought out. For instance, the triadic dialogue findings by Epp, et. al. (2009).

Strategies in Making Course Meaningful for Students Practice:

- Facilitators use strategies to connect and engage with students in conversations about the content and non-content related topics to form a relationship with each student.
- Facilitators are encourage to support communication between students and seek out and make available for variety of supplemental support tools to meet the diverse needs of students.
- In providing support, facilitators or teachers monitor student progress closely and interact with students to determine where gaps in knowledge may exist.

Communication & Community Strategy

- Facilitators, or teachers facilitate the formation of community by encouraging content and non-content related conversations among students.
- Teachers interact with students using multiple channels of communication (telephone, IM, etc provide support. Teachers model what formal online communication looks like in discussion boards and emails.
- Teachers also must effectively monitor the tone and emotion of their communications with students

Ability to Develop Positive and Constructive Feedback

- Facilitator to use three facilitation strategies such as inspirational, practice oriented, and highly structured to overcome instructor dominated facilitation for student-led discussion online (Baran, & et.al., 2009).
- Facilitator's ability to depersonalize of text message to be critically thought out before delivery (Epp, & et. al.2009).
- Facilitator's ability to distinguish student's de-motivated factors, follow up on prompt responses, queries, problem solving, and flexible delivery of the text medium through computer mediated (Cavanaugh, et. al. 2009).

- Facilitator's ability in using social role involving "reinforcement of good discussion behaviors through welcoming messages and prompt feedback with a positive tone" (Baran, et.al., 2009, p.340).

Online Classroom Evaluation Checklist (Hosie, & et.al., 2005)

- *Predictive Evaluation:* Useful screening device for evaluating online courseware an assessment of the quality and potential of a software application before it is used with students.
- *ECU Framework for evaluating quality materials online:* The main ideas: pedogogies, resources, and delivery strategies. Consistent assessment, checklist for critical elements of effective learning, capacity to investigate the potential effectiveness of online units, checklist of strength and weaknesses, peer evaluations.
- *Context-bound Evaluation:* Powerful and valuable addition to traditional forms of evaluation.
- *Courseware evaluation:* a sound instructional design.

REFERENCES

- Ali, A. (2003). Instructional design and online instruction: Practices and perception. *Techtrends*, 47(5), 42-45. http://proxy1.ncu.edu/login?url=http://search.ebscohost.com/login.aspx?direct=true&db=eric&AN=EJ678107&site=eds-live

- Baghdadi, Z. D. (2011). Best practices in online education: Online instructors, courses, and administrators. *Turkish Online Journal Of Distance Education*, 12(3) 109-117. http://proxy1.ncu.edu/login?url=http://search.ebscohost.com/login.aspx?direct=true&db=eric&AN=EJ965061&site=eds-live

- Baran, E., & Correia, A. (2009). Student-led facilitation strategies in online discussions. *Distance Education*, 30(3), 339-361. http://proxy1.ncu.edu/login?url=http://search.ebscohost.com/login.aspx?direct=true&db=ehh&AN=44500355&site=eds-live

- DiPietro, M., Ferdig, R. E., Black, E. W., & Presto, M. (2010). Best practices in teaching K-12 online: Lessons learned from Michigan virtual school teachers. *Journal Of Interactive Online Learning*, 9(3), 10-35. http://proxy1.ncu.edu/login?url=http://search.ebscohost.com/login.aspx?direct=true&db=eric&AN=EJ938843&site=eds-live

- Hosie, P., Schibeci, R., & Backhaus, A. (2005). A framework and checklists for evaluating online learning in higher education. *Assessment and Evaluation in Higher Education.* http://proxy1.ncu.edu/login?url=http://search.ebscohost.com/login.aspx?direct=true&db=ehh&AN=18021600&site=eds-live

- Maurino, P., Federman, F., & Greenwald, L. (2008). Online threaded discussions: Purposes, goals, and objectives. *Journal Of Educational Technology Systems*, 36(2), 129-143. http://proxy1.ncu.edu/login?url=http://search.ebscohost.com/login.aspx?direct=true&db=ehh&AN=31161447&site=eds-live

- Merrill, H. S. 2003 Best practices for online facilitation. *Adult Learning*, 14(2), 13. http://proxy1.ncu.edu/login?url=http://search.ebscohost.com/login.aspx?direct=true&db=ehh&AN=20961707&site=eds-live

- Ormiston, M. (2011). Creating a digital-rich classroom. Bloomington, IN: Solution Tree

- Press. Pappas, M. L. (2007). Tools for the assessment of learning. *School Library Media Activities Monthly*, 23(9), 21-25.http://proxy1.ncu.edu/login?url=http://search.ebscohost.com/login.aspx?direct=true&db=eric&AN=EJ784680&site=eds-live

DR. SOFIA LAURDEN DAVIS' BIOGRAPHY

Sofia Laurden Davis is a PhD in Human Services specialized in Management in Nonprofit Agencies and Leadership graduated in April 2014 from Capella University. Dr. Davis is currently an Independent Contractor as mortgage closer/signer with mortgage, bank, law and title companies function as a Certified Signing Specialist/Notary Public. She has 2 sons, Rhoss (Junjun) 38, and Danny (Jr) 33 years of age. Both sons are married. Currently, Dr. Davis has 5 grandchildren. Danny (JR) is a medical doctor graduated his doctorate at Florida State University (FSU). Dr. Davis was divorced in 1998 and remarried in 2004 to a wonderful man who is her confidante all along. His name is Tom.

Since 1989, Dr. Sofia L. Davis worked in banking and real estate industries. Beginning of year 2000, she became an Independent Contractor working part time while pursuing her education. Currently, she is an entrepreneur, a previous volunteer of Guardian Ad Litem serves as a Certified Court Officer as the voice for neglected and abused children in the area, a mentor for GAL volunteers, and she taught 4th & 5th religious education in the church she attended. She teached art classes and offers a "Courtesy Art Classes" and she travels to art students' selected location, and or class can be held in her own Fine Art Studio. She is an Independent Contractor performing signings for mortgage, bank and title companies.

After awarded her PhD in 2014 at Capella Univeristy she attended Certification in Teaching Online with Northcentral University. In 2006 she graduated her Master's degree in Human Resource Management from University of Phoenix. She has a Bachelor's degree major in Art History, and Studio Art at Georgian Court University in New Jersey graduated in 2004, and an Associates degree in Liberal Arts doubled with Photography at Brookdale Community College graduated in 2000. She moved from Bricktown New Jersey to Bonifay Florida in 2004. The same year, she developed a 501 C3 organization named Bonifay Guild for the Arts, Inc. which in year 2010 this organization was renamed to Laurden-Davis & Associates sole proprietorship consists of Mobile Signing Agent, Notary Public, Fine Art Studio, Online Art Gallery, and Rental Properties. Dr. Davis developed a year book for her previous organization titled, "Memorable Moments of Bonifay Guild for the Arts, Inc. Part 1" The book has 110 pages of compiled photos, stories, and activities of Bonifay Guild for the Arts, Inc. The year book copies were placed at Chambers of Commerce, and libraries for previous BGA and LDA members' keepsake.

Dr. Sofia Laurden Davis plan to teach online, and engage in research community. Currently Dr. Davis is a Notary Public, Signing Agent and she plans to continue writing books, teaching fine art categorize as an independent contractor. After she graduated with PhD at Capella University Dr. Davis published her dissertation in April 2014 with ProQuest, manuscript number #3617336. Her second book titled "Through the Lens of the World Health Crisis Part 1 was published through iUniverse.com. The third book was published through Xlibris Publishing Company titled "The Study of Family-Owned and Operated Organizations. Also, Dr. Davis, manuscript was discovered by Scholar's Press through Capella University's website and was one of the few selected manuscript to be published. The book can be transformed into 7 world languages. Thank you.

REFERENCES

Ali, A. (2003). Instructional design and online instruction: Practices and perception. *Techtrends*, 47(5), 42-45. http://proxy1.ncu.edu/login?url=http://search.ebscohost.com/login.aspx?direct=true&db=eric&AN=EJ678107&site=eds-live

Baghdadi, Z. D. (2011). Best practices in online education: Online instructors, courses, and administrators. *Turkish Online Journal Of Distance Education*, 12(3) 109-117. http://proxy1.ncu.edu/login?url=http://search.ebscohost.com/login.aspx?direct=true&db=eric&AN=EJ965061&site=eds-live

Brindley, J. E., Walti, C., and Blaschke, L. M. (2009). International Review of Research in Open and Distance Learning, Vol. 10, Issue 3, Database: Directory of Open Access Journals.

Belair, M. (2012). The investigation of virtual school communications. *Techtrends: Linking Research And Practice To Improve Learning*, 56(4), 26-33. ://proxy1.ncu.edu/login?url=http://search.ebscohost.com/login.aspx?direct=true&db=ehh&AN=77569810&site=eds-live

Bliss, C. A., & Lawrence, B. (2009). From posts to patterns: A metric to characterize discussion board activity in online courses. *Journal of Asynchronous Learning Networks*,13(2), 15-32. http://proxy1.ncu.edu/login?url=http://search.ebscohost.com/login.aspx?direct=true&db=eric&AN=EJ862344&site=eds-live

Brindley, J. E., Walti, C., & Blaschke, L. M. (2009). Creating effective collaborative learning groups in an online environment. *International Review of Research in Open and Distance Learning*, 10(3). http://proxy1.ncu.edu/login?url=http://search.ebscohost.com/login.aspx?direct=true&db=eric&AN=EJ847776&site=eds-live

Brooks, C. F., & Bippus, A. M. (2012). Underscoring the social nature of classrooms by Examining the amount of virtual talk across online and blended college courses. *European Journal of Open, Distance and E-Learning*, 1. http://eric.ed.gov/?id=EJ979602

Burdett, J. (2007). Degrees of separation—Balancing intervention and independence in group work assignments. *Australian Educational Researcher,* 34(1), 55-71. http://proxy1.ncu.edu/login?url=http://search. ebscohost.com/login.aspx?direct=true&db=eric&AN=EJ766604&site= eds-live

Chaves, C. A. (2009). On-line course curricula and interactional strategies: The foundations and extensions to adult e-learning communities European. *Journal of Open, Distance and E-Learning,* 1. http://eric. ed.gov/?id=EJ911758

Dennen, V. (2005). From message posting to learning Dialogues: Factors affecting Learner Participation in Asynchronous Discussion. *Discussion. Distance Education*, 26(1), 127-148. http://proxy1.ncu.edu/login?url=http:// search.ebscohost.com/login.aspx?direct=true&db=ehh&AN=33185139&s ite=eds-live

DiPietro, M., Ferdig, R. E., Black, E. W., & Presto, M. (2010). Best practices in teaching K-12 online: Lessons learned from Michigan virtual school teachers. *Journal Of Interactive Online Learning*, 9(3), 10-35. http://proxy1. ncu.edu/login?url=http://search.ebscohost.com/login.aspx?direct=true&db =eric&AN=EJ938843&site=eds-live

Gardner, H., (2010). Five minds for the future. In Bellanca J., Brandt, R., 21st century skills: Rethinking how students learn. (p.9). Morton Street, Bloomington, IN 47404.

Gardner, H., (2008). *Five minds for the future.* Boston, Massachusetts, Harvard Business School Publishing.

Fisher, D., and Frey, N., (2010). Preparing students for mastery of 21st century skills. In Bellanca J.,Brandt, R., 21st century skills: Rethinking how students learn. (pp. 225-228). Morton Street, Bloomington, IN 47404.

Fogarty, R. and Pete, B.M. (2010). The singapore vision; teach less, learn more. In Bellanca J., Brandt, R., 21st century skills: Rethinking how student learn. (p.97). Bloomington, IN. Solution Tree Press.

Hamann, K., Pollock, P. H., & Wilson, B. M. (2009). Learning from "listening" to peers in online political science classes. *Journal of Political Science Education*, 5(1), 1-11. http://proxy1.ncu.edu/login?url=http://search.ebscohost.com/login.aspx?direct=true&db=ehh&AN=36359661&site=eds-live

Heydenberk, R., & Heydenberk, W. R. (2007). The conflict resolution connection: Increasing school attachment in cooperative classroom communities. *Reclaiming Children And Youth: The Journal Of Strength-Based Interventions*, 16(3), 18-22. http://proxy1.ncu.edu/login?url=http://search.ebscohost.com/login.as px?direct=true&db=ehh&AN=27760357&site=eds-live

Hu, H., & Gramling, J. (2009). Learning strategies for success in a web-based course: A descriptive exploration. *Quarterly Review Of Distance Education*, 10(2), 123-134. http://proxy1.ncu.edu/login?url=http://search.ebscohost.com/login.aspx?direct=true&db=asx&AN=44895674&site=eds-live

Jahng, N., & Bullen, M. (2012). Exploring group forming strategies by examining participation behaviours during whole class discussions European. *Journal of Open, Distance and E-Learning*, 1. http://eric.ed.gov/?id=EJ979606

Jones, I. M. (2011). Can you see me now? Defining teaching presence in the online classroom Through building a learning community. *Journal of Legal Studies Education*, 28(1), 67-116. http://proxy1.ncu.edu/login?url=http://search.ebscohost.com/login.aspx?direct=true&db=eric&AN=EJ916830&site=eds-live

Lemke, C., (2010). Innovation through technology. In Bellanca J., Brandt, R., 21st century skills: Rethinking how students learn. (p. 244). Morton Street, Bloomington, IN 47404.

Merrill, H. S. 2003 Best practices for online facilitation. *Adult Learning*, 14(2), 13.http://proxy1.ncu.edu/login?url=http://search.ebscohost.com/login.aspx?direct=true&db=ehh&AN=20961707&site=eds-live

Meyer, K. A. (2007). Does feedback influence learner postings to online discussions? *Journal of Educators Online*, 4(1). http://www.thejeo.com/Archives/Volume4Number1/MeyerFinal.pdf

Morgan, T. (2011). Online classroom or community-in-the-making? instructor conceptualizations and teaching presence in international online contexts *Journal of Distance Education*, 25(1). http://proxy1.ncu.edu/login?url=http://search.ebscohost.com/login.aspx?direct=true&db=ehh&AN=75153218&site=eds-live

Nair, S. P. (2012). Towards understanding the successful learner: A case study of IGNOU. *Turkish Online Journal of Distance Education*, 13(2), 322-335. http://proxy1.ncu.edu/login?url=http://search.ebscohost.com/login.aspx?direct=true&db=eric&AN=EJ983665&site=eds-live

Nandi, D., Hamilton, M., Chang, S., & Balbo, S. (2012). Evaluating quality in online asynchronous interactions between students and discussion facilitators. *Australasian Journal of Educational Technology*, 28(4), 684-702. http://proxy1.ncu.edu/login?url=http://search.ebscohost.com/login.aspx?direct=true&db=ehh&AN=77978505&site=eds-live

Nie, M., Armellini, A., Witthaus, G., & Barklamb, K. (2011). How do E-book readers enhance learning opportunities for distance work-based learners? *Research in Learning Technology*, 19(1), 19-38. http://proxy1.ncu.edu/login?url=http://search.ebscohost.com/login.aspx?direct=true&db=ehh&AN=65255977&site=ehost-live

O'Neill, S., Scott, M., & Conboy, K. (2011). A delphi study on collaborative learning in distance education:The faculty perspective. B*ritish Journal of Educational Technology*, 42(6), 939-949. http://proxy1.ncu.edu/login?url=http://search.ebscohost.com/login.aspx?direct=true&db=ehh&AN=66716188&site=eds-live

Pearlman, B., (2010). Designing new learning environments to support 21st century skills. In Bellanca J., Brandt, R., 21st century skills:Rethinking how students learn. (p.118). Morton Street, Bloomington, IN 47404.

Quillerous, E. (2011). Increased technology provision and learning: Giving more for nothing? *International Review of Research in Open and Distance Learning,* 12(6), 178-197. http://proxy1.ncu.edu/login?url=http://search.ebscohost.com/login.aspx?direct=true&db=eric&AN=EJ964058&site=eds-live

Radovan, M. (2011). The relation between distance students' motivation, their use of learning strategies, and academic success. *Turkish Online Journal of Educational Technology - TOJET,* 10(1), 216-222. http://proxy1.ncu.edu/login?url=http://search.ebscohost.com/login.aspx?direct=true&db=eric&AN=EJ926571&site=eds-live

Rasmussen, K. L., Nichols, J., & Ferguson, F. (2006). It's a new world: Multiculturalism in a virtual environment. *Distance Education,* 27(2), 265-278. http://proxy1.ncu.edu/login?url=http://search.ebscohost.com/login.aspx?direct=true& db=ehh&AN=21806767&site=eds-live

Rhode, J. F. (2009). Interaction equivalency in self-paced online learning environments: An exploration of learner preferences. *International Review of Research in Open and Distance Learning,* 10(1). http://proxy1.ncu.edu/login?url=http://search.ebscohost.com/login.aspx?direct=true&db=eric&AN=EJ831712&site=eds-live

Sher, A. (2009). Assessing the relationship of student-instructor and student-learner interaction to learner learning and satisfaction in web-based online learning environment. *Journal Of Interactive Online Learning,* 8(2), 102-120. http://www.ncolr.org/jiol/issues/pdf/8.2.1.pdf

Simpson, O., (2008). Motivating learners in open and distance learning: do we need a new theory of learner support? The Open University, Vol 23, No.3 November 2008, 159-170. DOI:10.1080/02680510802419979.

Stone, S. J., & Chapman, D. D. (2006). Instructor presence in the online classroom. http://eric.ed.gov/?id=ED492845

Wang, Y., & Chen, D. (2010). Promoting spontaneous facilitation in online discussions: Designing object and ground rules. *Educational Media International,* 47(3) 247-262. http://proxy1.ncu.edu/login?url=http://search.

ebscohost.com/login.aspx?direct=true&db=ehh&AN=55053957&site=
eds-live

Walker, K. (2004). Activity systems and conflict resolution in an online professional communication course. *Business Communication Quarterly*, 67(2), 182-197. http://proxy1.ncu.edu/login?url=http://search.ebscohost. com/login.as px?direct=true&db=bth&AN=13871725&site=eds-live

Wickersham, L. E., & McGee, P. (2008). Perceptions of satisfaction and deeper learning in an online course. *Quarterly Review of Distance Education*, 9(1), 73-83. http://proxy1.ncu.edu/login?url=http://search. ebscohost.com/login.aspx?direct=true&db=eric&AN=EJ875089&site= eds-live

Wise, A., Saghafian, M., & Padmanabhan, P. (2012). Towards more precise design guidance: Specifying and testing the functions of assigned learner roles in online discussions. *Educational Technology Research and Development*, 60(1), http://proxy1.ncu.edu/login?url=http://search. ebscohost.com/login.aspx?direct=true&db=eric&AN=EJ954585&site= eds-live

Zen, D. (2008). How to be an effective online instructor. http://files.eric. ed.gov/fulltext/ED502683.pdf

Zhang, W., Perris, K., & Yeung, L. (2005).Online tutorial support in open and distance learning: Students' perceptions. *British Journal of Educational Technology*, 6(5), 789-804. http://proxy1.ncu.edu/login?url=http://search. ebscohost.com/login.aspx?direct=true&db=ehh&AN=17908846&site= eds-live

BIBLIOGRAPHY

Chaves, C. A. (2009). On-line course curricula and interactional strategies: The foundations and extensions to adult e-learning communities European. *Journal of Open, Distance and E-Learning,* 1. http://eric.ed.gov/?id=EJ911758

The article highlights the online curriculum interaction model and information through foundational philosophical, theoretical, research based result and professional experiences. For examples, the four levels of interactions stages: ascending level of interaction, initial course content (academic), student-peer, and instructor-student interaction. (p.1).

Quillerou, E. (2011). Increased technology provision and learning: Giving more for nothing? *International Review of Research in Open and Distance Learning,* 12(6), 178-197. http://proxy1.ncu.edu/login?url=http://search.ebscohost.com/login.aspx?direct=true&db=eric&AN=EJ964058&site=eds-live

Due to technology use for teaching and learning, Quillerous's research findings stated that "students' specific needs or situations need to be considered for the design of an effective learning toolbox" (p.169).

Rasmussen, K. L., Nichols, J., & Ferguson, F. (2006). It's a new world: Multiculturalism in a virtual environment. *Distance Education,* 27(2), 265-278. http://proxy1.ncu.edu/login?url=http://search.ebscohost.com/login.aspx?direct=true&db=ehh&AN=21806767&site=eds-live

Diversity and multiculturalism matters because of globalization. Therefore, exploration and investigation in this type of cultural change affect the people, society and the community. It affects businesses and the educational systems. We are now able to offer product and services globally that we need to understand the needs of each individual and develop strategies to bridge multicultural gaps.

Wickersham, L. E., & McGee, P. (2008). Perceptions of satisfaction and deeper learning in an online course. *Quarterly Review of Distance Education, 9*(1), 73-83. http://proxy1.ncu.edu/login?url=http://search.ebscohost.com/login.aspx?direct=true&db=eric&AN=EJ875089&site=eds-live

With the comparison between face-to-face and online learning environment that the findings revealed no difference unless students' application on DLP and learner's satisfaction methods are applied in an online learning environment.

www.ingramcontent.com/pod-product-compliance
Lightning Source LLC
Chambersburg PA
CBHW051254050326
40689CB00007B/1197